Hoof Beats and Hummingbirds

A life time of being outsmarted by "dumb animals"

Sandra M. Packard

Dedication

For my husband, Richard, who believes in me even when I don't believe in myself. Honey, could you please feed the dog?

Table of Contents

Acknowledgments

I would like to thank Karen Condon, a friend and writer who, God bless her, seems to think I'm as funny as she is. Without her enthusiasm I would have quit on this project many times.

I would also like to thank Ed McCarthy, a friend, writer, and neighbor who once made my year by referring to me as a "fellow author." Without his encouragement and guidance I would have truly not known how to proceed.

I am also grateful to Becca Guilbault-Tripplett, a friend who took my author's photo and is a professional photographer. Becca is also a professional horse trainer and riding instructor as well as an actress and stuntwoman.

I would like to thank my husband, Richard, who has not only stuck by me and believed in me for forty-four years, but has never once served me with divorce papers. The man deserves a medal, not an acknowledgment.

I would also like to show gratitude to both of my wonderful children, Andrea and Bryan, both of whom I admire and love beyond mere words. I would also like to explain to them that this book is not all about them because, after all, unlike the pets, they could sue.

Finally, I would like to acknowledge everyone at CreateSpace who allows voices to be heard that otherwise would have been silent. In most cases, this is a good thing.

Chapter 1

Introduction

It had been a lovely spring day, but as so often happens in New England, the night was shaping up ominously—that is, if you don't like thunderstorms. I don't. The sky had darkened long before nightfall, and the winds had increased alarmingly. Most, though not all, of the animals in our lives were also inclined to dislike this kind of weather. Perhaps they got it from me. They sure didn't get if from my husband, Richard.

I prefer to think the ones that had it were born with it. I have enough guilt about the fears and foibles of my children. Anyway, not long after, I brought home a feral kitten—black and white and no bigger than a minute—a thunderstorm broke in the middle of the night. I named the kitten "Lil' Bitty," because that is what he was. My husband indulged me, but would only call him Bitty, for what I suspect were masculine reasons.

Shortly after the storm started, I felt a rush of air and saw a blur as I opened one half-asleep eye. A shivering ball of fur launched itself at me. I was lying on my side, and he ended up curled under my neck. At this time, we were also the loving owners of a 150-pound bullmastiff named Luther. We never allowed any of our pets on the furniture, never mind the bed. Luther was a fine fellow and followed the rules. At most, he would sleep beside the bed, usually on Richard's side. But when Bitty catapulted himself into me, Luther rose from his resting place walked around the bed and stared at me with accusing eyes. He wasn't afraid of thunder or lighting, but he had a firm grasp on what was fair.

"Okay," I sighed, but pointed firmly to the foot of the bed.

He didn't jump but rather climbed aboard as gracefully as a ballerina. A flash of light and a cringe-inducing boom rang out that woke even my heavily sleeping husband. He rolled over and threw a reassuring arm around my shoulder. We had been married for over thirty years at that point, so he was pretty much imperturbable. However, his reassuring gesture caused his hand to end up in a thick ball of fur under my chin.

"Um, honey, what *is* that?"

"The cat."

He glanced at the floor on his side of the bed.

"Where's the dog?"

I pointed to the bottom of the bed. Rich sighed and settled back to sleep muttering, "Boy I'm glad we're boarding the horse."

I wanted this to be about the animals in our lives, all of which have been special and loved and for some reason a little odd. Or perhaps we've been the odd ones because over our forty-plus-year marriage we have collected an eclectic group of pets that I hesitate to say we've owned, since it often has seemed the other way around.

The first one in our married life was a cat named Flower. We were living in a third-floor apartment in Worcester, Massachusetts. A family member gave the cat to us, which was why we had to keep her. This was not a kitten, mind you, but a full-grown, born-and-living-in-the-wild cat. Neither of us knew anything about feral cats. This was a long time ago. I don't remember much about her except that she absolutely hated us. Both of us. And we were all she had. She would hiss, growl, and meow constantly, day and night. There was no evidence she ever slept. She even growled between bites of food. Yes, we fed and watered her and would have petted her if she'd let us. She didn't.

Our apartment building was old, not charming old, just old, cheap, and rundown. The bedroom light was turned on and off by a chain hanging from the light over the bed. One night, I felt a pressure on my chest and heard an unearthly, rumbling noise. I opened my eyes and stared straight into two slanted yellow eyes glaring back at me. I screamed and yanked the light on. The cat fled. After that we slept with the door shut.

This was my first experience with a feral cat; obviously, it would not be my last. At the time I just couldn't understand her apparent loathing. One day, the building owner arrived to fix a leak in the pipes. As he knocked on our door, the strict "no pets" clause in our lease flashed through my mind. This was it, our ticket out, now we would have to get rid of her. When I opened the door, Flower launched herself at the poor man. I assumed murder was on her mind. Besides Rich and me, she didn't like anyone else, either. He caught her in mid-leap and cradled her in his arms. At that point, she began to purr. Purr! I didn't even know she could.

"What a sweet kitty."

Okay, if you like the cat from hell, it was fine by me.

"I know we're not supposed to have pets here," I began.

"Oh, that's okay," he said. "She can stay. Look how she's licking my fingers. She's so cute."

I suspected she might just be tasting him before the kill, but I saw the lease option fading away before my eyes. I tried another tactic.

"She really seems to like you. Maybe you would want to take her?"

"I could never take your darling kitty away from you."

"Of course you could. She scares the crap out of us."

"What?"

"Nothing." I couldn't understand the situation myself, much less explain it.

He left; the cat stayed and immediately reverted to her old self. Then one humid day, we opened our windows in an attempt to get a breeze. We not only didn't have air-conditioning, but we didn't have screens. Flower jumped onto the windowsill. She didn't look like she was looking for a place to relax. She never relaxed.

I felt my stomach tighten, and I called to Richard, "My God, Flower is going to jump!"

She looked like she was measuring the distance from the third-floor window to the ground and freedom.

"She won't jump, it's too high."

At that, she threw a disdainful glance at us (not the first) and launched herself into space. We rushed to the window and looked out. She not only survived the jump, but she "stuck the landing," as they say in the Olympics. She glanced up at our distraught faces and calmly strutted away. I've heard, as almost everyone has, that cats always land on their feet; however, I wouldn't have believed this if I hadn't seen it. We know she survived unhurt because, for as long as we lived in that apartment, we would hear her growling and meowing throughout the night. We put out food for her, and she ate it, or something did, but she never stepped foot in our apartment again. I have no idea what eventually happened to her. Since this was over forty years ago, I guess she would have died of natural causes by now. Or maybe she tracked down the building owner and they lived happily together for many years. I'd like to think so.

We only lived in that apartment for a year, but in that period of time, we acquired another cat, this one quite sweet, that we would keep for years and a German shepherd puppy. There was still the "no pets" clause in the lease, but we didn't think anyone would notice. We had to find another home for the puppy because, despite our optimism, well, people noticed. This one year in which we acquired three pets set a pattern for the future.

As a child, I had many animals, although mostly of the smaller variety: canaries, parakeets, rabbits, baby chicks, hamsters, cats, and a couple of dogs. We didn't live in the country, but we had a house with a yard. It wasn't exactly a city, but a small town. I guess today you would call it the suburbs, but that word hadn't been coined yet. And the house we lived in didn't seem grand enough for that title.

Both of my parents came from tenements in the city, and neither had much experience with animals. That could explain the short life span of some of the ones we had. Or if they lived too long, why they always went to that mythical farm where they could romp and play with other animals and basically be off my parents' nerves. One summer evening, my father brought my sister and me each a baby rabbit. While getting them pellets at the feed store, he won twelve baby chicks in a raffle. To my knowledge, this is the only thing he ever won in his entire life. They didn't have lotteries in those days. So he won chickens. My parents hadn't a clue as to how to care for them.

They had good intentions, giving them food and water; however, they didn't know baby chicks needed a heating lamp to keep them sufficiently warm. One by one, each little chick passed away. Every single time, my sister and I wailed and carried on. My father was a drinking man, but I honestly couldn't pinpoint it to this particular event.

Richard's childhood was a bit different. He came from a family with five children. He said, as did all his siblings, that his mother didn't like animals. They had a dog for a short period of time, but that was it.

I remember a day when my mother-in-law was visiting. While sitting on our couch, she literally fell all over our current dog, a lovely white German shepherd. She petted it, cooed to it, and at one point, even took off her shoes to run her toes through the dog's luxurious fur.

More than a little amazed, I blurted, "I thought you didn't like animals."

"Who told you that?"

It seemed unkind to say "everyone," so my husband took the fall when I answered. "Richard said you never allowed them to have pets."

"Oh, for God's sake, I love animals, especially dogs. But I had five children. When I finally brought a dog home, they taunted and teased the poor thing so much he started to nip, and we had to get rid of him."

Poor slandered Mom, but that's a story for another time. Maybe I'll write it when everyone who would be inclined to sue has passed away—assuming I'm still here. At any rate, Richard had minimal exposure to the animal kingdom. That all changed when he met me. To the surprise of both of us, he had a heart twice as soft as mine.

When it came to animals—or the children and me, for that matter—he didn't always do the right thing. No one does. Sometimes it's hard to figure out what the right thing even is. But he almost always does the kind thing. There are not very many people you can say that about. I'm glad I'm married to one of them.

Chapter 2
Tanya

Our first child was a boy who we named Bryan. By this time, we had moved from our apartment in Worcester, Massachusetts, to another apartment in Coventry, Rhode Island. Other than the sweet cat from our Worcester apartment who was named Pinky—he wasn't pink, but his nose was—this was a relatively pet-free time. When we moved into our first house a year after Bryan was born, we of course took Pinky along. The house we found was only about ten minutes by car from the apartment. This turned out to be lucky for Pinky. Shortly after we moved into the house, he disappeared. Although we searched and searched, we eventually had to give up. About three weeks later, our landlord's wife called to say our cat was at our apartment's back door.

Our landlord and his wife were lovely people. They couldn't do enough for us when we moved in. Although they also had requested no pets, we were up front about the cat. They made an exception, which was lucky because it would have been a deal breaker and I loved the apartment. It was an older home that had been turned into a duplex. They lived on one side; we lived on the other.

The landlord was over ninety years old, and his wife was eighty-five. They not only allowed us to have the cat, but they grew very fond of him. We had an adjoining basement, separated only by a door. Whenever I put the cat out, I would be mystified to find him back inside within minutes. Finally, I caught the landlord's wife letting him in through the cellar. She thought it was mean to put him out.

At any rate, they had no way of knowing the cat had disappeared from his new home. We had taken Pinky by car and were incredulous to think he could have found his way back to our old apartment. To be honest, we thought it was a cat that might have looked like ours. We only went over to see it to be nice. I mean, these people were really old, and they certainly meant well.

When we pulled into the driveway, our landlady was sitting on the front porch in her rocking chair. Pinky was in her lap. He didn't look thin or even hungry, and his fur was as shiny as ever. Cats never fail to amaze me. We kept Pinky for another year or so and then gave him to a good home. A family member had lost his cat of many years and was distraught. Our family was expanding, and we were thinking of getting a dog. It seemed like the right thing to do. Although, to be honest, even though his new home was far away in a different state, I half expected him to show up at our door one day.

Two and a half years after Bryan, we had a second baby, this time a girl we named Andrea. We had been thinking of getting a dog, and now with the new baby, it only seemed right to get Bryan a dog. That way he would have something of his very own to take care of. He was about three years old at the time. The idea of his actually taking care of a dog was optimistic to say the least, but that never stopped us before.

I always liked German shepherds. My first paycheck went to purchase a purebred puppy. He lived up to all my expectations. He was smart and loyal and just plain gorgeous. With two small children, finances were tight. A purebred seemed out of reach to us; however, we did see white German shepherds for sale for a fraction of the normal price. Being white, they would be disqualified from shows and therefore not much in demand for breeding. The important part was they would have all the same personality traits as a regular German shepherd. That was the kind of dog I wanted around my children.

We went to a kennel that bred only white shepherds. I didn't understand why at the time. Their price would rise over the years as they became popular pets, so I guess the breeders were on the right track. As far as I know, white Shepherds are still disqualified from dog shows, although they are actually as beautiful—some think more beautiful—as the normally colored black, tan, and brown dogs.

The one we chose was about five months old, a pure white female with enormous soft brown eyes. She was already named, and she had a sexier name than mine. I tried not to hold that against her. Her name was

Tanya. We kept the name so as not to confuse the dog. She rode home in the front seat with us. Cars had bench seats in those days. Every time we went under an overpass or bridge, she would duck her head. I don't know why. We never had another dog with that particular quirk. They all had one quirk or another, though, some more unique than others. Some were just one big living, breathing quirk. We'll get to that later.

Tanya was already housebroken when we got her. Training her was a snap. She was very intelligent and eager to please. She bonded immediately with her diminutive owner. Things worked out pretty much as we planned—almost. As the years started to pass, we discovered that Bryan not only had asthma, but he had allergies.

He was tested, and although he didn't test positive specifically for dogs, his pediatrician thought it was a poor idea to have the dog sleep in the same room with him—our son's room, not the pediatrician's, but I guess you figured that part out. Tanya had always slept in Bryan's room, and explaining allergies to animals or children is impossible. Trust me on this one.

We started putting the dog to bed on a rug in the dining room after Bryan went to bed. She was very obedient, and when told to "go to your rug and lie down," she did so with no quarrel. Sometimes she was there in the morning. Sometimes she was back in my son's room. When I got up one night to go to the bathroom, I ran into her sneaking down the hall. This was a three-bedroom raised ranch with a narrow hall that had all three bedrooms running off it. As soon as Tanya saw me, she froze. She refused to make eye contact. That's when I realized she was trying to blend into her surroundings—a sixty-five-pound white German shepherd in a narrow hallway hoping with all her might that I wouldn't notice her.

After this incident, we began to put a leash on Tanya at bedtime and attach the other end to the dining room table. That way she could rest comfortably on her rug, but couldn't roam. This resulted in soft whining from the dog and muffled sobs from Bryan. Rich and I lay awake in bed, listening, feeling like two really horrible subhuman beings. However, when you are a parent, you have to do the responsible—or in this case, really crappy—thing. So these sleeping arrangements would remain for the rest of Tanya's life. We all eventually became exhausted and fell asleep.

Another problem Tanya had was a touchy digestive system. This could have been brought about by the stress of her sleeping arrangements, but let's not dwell on that. One problem that was definitely not caused by stress was the worms she threw up all over the kitchen floor. I had heard of dogs having worms before, but this was my first experience with them. Gross doesn't even begin to describe it. I called the veterinarian, and the receptionist said they had an opening the following week. I don't usually think of myself as assertive, but as I wrestled with the phone (they had cords connected to the walls in those days) the dog, and my two children, all the time keeping a wary eye on the worms, I heard myself scream into the phone, "You'll see her NOW!" They agreed.

We almost never left the kids with a babysitter. In fact, Andrea refused to be left. She was a tiny little thing and cute as a button, but she had the two most powerful lungs ever heard in North America. Really. Her shrieking could make your ears bleed, and shriek is what she did whenever we left her.

Consequently, we almost never did, and if we did, we never got the same babysitter back for a second go of it. Now I had to impose on a neighbor to watch both children while I drove the dog to the veterinarian's office, which was in a different town. I never could have handled all three of them in the car. So as Tanya and I left, I could hear my baby daughter screaming like she was being murdered, and I had no choice but to go.

At this time, I should tell you I wasn't a good driver, never was, and still am not, and I only had a vague idea of where the veterinarian's office was located. To make matters worse, traffic was horrible. Also, I had a nauseous dog hanging her head over my shoulder from the backseat making the occasional gagging noise.

When we finally got there, I grabbed Tanya's leash and rushed into the office. I held the leash loosely because Tanya was never a problem. She was friendly with everyone—people and animals. And, frankly, I wasn't entirely with it at this point. It is never good to let your guard down. The loose leash allowed Tanya to jump onto the waiting room bench, where a rather large woman sat with a very tiny dog in her lap. The two of them looked like a cliché. Tanya's intention was to make another friend. That wasn't going to happen.

The women rose, dog in hand, and shouted to the receptionist, "I'll wait my turn in my car, since you let people in here who can't control their animals."

Tanya wagged her tail tentatively, and I slunk to a nearby seat and sat in shame for the first (but not the last) time because of an animal. When it was our turn, the vet who examined Tanya burst out laughing. When he tried to check her, she kept licking his glasses and fogging them up.

"What a great dog!" he said.

"You want her?"

"What?"

"Never mind."

The worm situation was one that could easily be cured with medication. Tanya and I returned home. As I rounded the corner to our house, I could hear Andrea still screaming. I'll admit now, for the first time, that it did cross my mind to drop the dog in front of the house and just keep driving. But I didn't. I loved them all—except the worms.

As time passed and Andrea grew, she, too, became attached to Tanya. She also became a stickler for the truth, which is why I have to include the incident about how I tried to throw lovely Tanya out the bathroom window. If I didn't, Andrea would never forgive me. I do have a defense, although, in retrospect, it does seem a bit thin. I was quite terrified of my in-laws. I think things were different in those days. Anyway, anytime they announced a plan to visit, I went on a frenzy of house cleaning. I was certain they were looking for just one puff of dirt so they could take my children away. I now know that wasn't they case, but it doesn't matter because that's what I believed at the time.

The house we bought was a new one. It was relatively easy to keep clean, but clean was not going to cut it in my mind. I usually washed and waxed the floors after the children went to bed. That way they would have time to dry before being walked on. The kitchen opened into the dining room, so both floors had to be scrubbed at the same time. The house was a split entry, with the front doorway opening into an entrance that had six stairs going up and six going down. That entrance was linoleum as well.

I scrubbed it on my hands and knees at the same time I did the kitchen and dining room.

On this particular night, I had just finished the final coat of wax when I heard Tanya start to whine. I think it was about 3:00 in the morning. Tanya was, for this one night, in our bedroom. One look at her desperate eyes and I knew she needed to go out. The sliding glass door was in the dining room, where there was a newly waxed floor. To get to the front door you had to go over the landing—more wet wax. The wax wasn't drying fast enough. It was clear that the dog couldn't wait.

This house had a split entry because it was built into a hill and the back was more or less at ground level. Keep that more or less in mind. I was desperately searching for a way to get the dog out of the house without ruining all my hard work. Then it came to me. The bathroom was in the back of the house, and the bathroom window must have been well less than half a story high. I thought I could just open the window and let Tanya jump out, do her business, and jump back in. I mean, come on people, we've all seen Lassie do it hundreds of times. Well, maybe not this exactly, but something equally difficult. And probably with an infant in her mouth and flames at her back.

I called Tanya into the bathroom and opened the window. I looked expectantly at her. She looked quizzically at me. She obviously was not on the same page. I tapped the windowsill, and she obligingly jumped up on her hind legs and rested her front legs on the windowsill. So far so good. I then encouraged her to "go" by clapping my hands and making insane happy noises. She glanced out the window and got down from the windowsill. This was not like her at all. She was usually so cooperative.

I peered out the window. I couldn't see anything, never mind the ground. After all, it was the middle of the night. I thought maybe she just needed a little more encouragement. This is where the shoving comes in. I tapped the windowsill, and she again jumped up, but not out. So I attempted to hoist her back end even with the front to make her descent easier. She started to struggle. Unlike me, she wasn't even a little crazy. I was trying to save my floors; she was trying to save her life. A dog has never bitten me, but if I ever deserved to be, it was that night.

Luckily for both of us, she was stronger than I was, and she not only refused another exit attempt, but she hastily left the bathroom. I gave in and called her to me. Amazingly, she came. Together, we walked through the kitchen, our feet sticking to the tacky wax, then through the dining room, more sticky and tacky, and I let her out. She ran out onto the deck and down four stairs to the yard to relieve herself. While I waited, it hit me—down four stairs? The back of the house couldn't have been level with the ground. I grabbed a flashlight and went into the yard. I flashed the light up to the bathroom window. I'm chagrined to tell you that would have been one hell of a jump. Tanya came back in, and I spent the rest of the night re-waxing the floors like I should have in the first place. Tanya never held my attempted dogacide against me. That's why you have to love dogs. They will forgive you anything.

All animal stories end the same way, and we all know how that is. The fact is people outlive animals—at least usually. I don't want to make this about endings because that diminishes the joy that all of the living, breathing additions to our family brought us. I will say that Tanya lived a normal life span. When the time came, she was gently "put to sleep" by her veterinarian. The only thing I feel I need to add about the end of her life is when it came about. She had gotten old and had severe arthritis among other problems. Bryan was extremely attached to her, as we all were, and making The Decision was tough. Although we knew the time had come, we kept putting it off.

Wherever Bryan was you could count on Tanya being with him. My son loves sports, particularly baseball. With apologies to him in advance, I have to say he wasn't very good. But it wasn't for the lack of trying or practice.

When his father wasn't home to pitch to him, he would throw the ball in the air and swing at it. He almost never hit it. One day, when he was in the backyard diligently executing batting practice alone, I heard the crack of the bat hitting the ball. Then, almost immediately, I heard another crack, a yelp of pain, and a shriek from my son. I rushed outside and saw Tanya on her side with Bryan cradling her head in his arms. He had hit a line drive straight at her head. She was too old and slow to get out of the way. When I got to her, there was no blood or visible dents in her head. She just seemed a little dazed. Within minutes, she could stand and seemed to be able to walk okay. Bryan's face was ashen.

"Mom, I didn't mean to hit her!"

I knew that. He was a sweet, kind child, and he loved her. Besides, he almost never hit the ball, never mind having any control over where it went. I didn't point that out because he was already distraught, and you don't kick people when they're down, especially your own children.

Instead, I said, "She's fine, Bry. I think it just scared her." I actually looked him right in the eye and said this, still hearing in my mind the horrid crack the ball made when it hit her head.

That night, after he went to bed, I sat on her rug with her. She placed her lovely head gently in my lap. I patted her head and stroked her silky ears. And then I begged her not to die. I told her I knew she was old and tired and in pain. I told her I didn't know if the blow to her head had done any damage or not. And I told her I knew she might not mind dying.

"But," I begged, "not tonight, Tanya, because if you die tonight, that little boy you love so much will never forgive himself."

And she didn't die that night or the next or anytime soon. She waited long enough so that even the guiltiest person couldn't connect her demise to an errant baseball. Thank you, Tanya. Thank you, God.

Sometime near the end of Tanya's life, we obtained another cat. This cat was named Booty because of his four white paws. Cats seemed to come and go at an alarming rate in our house. We usually didn't seek them out. They just showed up, we fed them, and they stayed, so we got them neutered and inoculated, and for various lengths of time, they lived with us. This particular cat was a good cat, and Tanya seemed to love him. I don't know if he loved her, but he sure enjoyed having her around.

We had a five-foot-high stockade fence around our house and yard. It descended to four feet as it reached the street. Don't ask me why. It had to do with some zoning regulation that I didn't understand at the time and still don't. Tanya never barked at people or charged the fence. I would say most people didn't even know she was there, but they did. One mother told me her little girl would always wave to Tanya on her way to school. One morning, when I was gazing out the window, I saw several children do just that. As a matter of fact, more people "knew" Tanya than knew us. We found out we were mainly known as the people with the beautiful, big, white dog. People who where more familiar with us knew us as Tanya's owners, or in my case, as Tanya's mother.

But back to Booty. If people knew there was a dog on the other side of that fence, animals didn't. This cat found out in short order that he could pick a fight with another cat, race home, jump over the fence, with the other cat chasing him, and then they both would be face to face with Tanya, at which point the other cat, or chaser, would have a kitty panic attack, do a 180-degree turn, and leap out of the yard. This sounds far-fetched, but it happened all the time and sometimes with more than one cat in pursuit. Tanya wouldn't have hurt any of them, but they didn't know that. Sometimes after they leapt out of the yard, our cat would jump to the top of the fence post and, for the cats that didn't keep running, would taunt them. If they came close, he would take a swipe at them, knowing they would not jump the fence a second time. I have several witnesses to this little kitty con game. He did it a lot.

The day after Tanya went to doggie heaven—and, yes, there is a doggie heaven—Booty came racing around the corner with three or four cats in hot pursuit. He jumped the fence, and the other cats stopped. They had apparently been through this game before. I was at the window at the time and knew there would be trouble because Booty jumped to the top of the fence and strutted and preened in front of them.

Finally, one cat got up his nerve and jumped the fence; our cat screeched around the corner of the house, with the other cat in hot pursuit, and to his amazement, and the other cat's surprise, there was...no dog. I was already out in the yard with a broom to ward off the chaser and shoo it away. Booty was cowering under the deck. I had to get down on my stomach and drag him out and into the house. I'm not an animal whisperer, and I don't pretend I can tell what they are thinking, but anyone could tell what this cat was thinking: "Hey, lady, what the hell did you do with my dog?"

He was never able to play that game again, and I don't think he ever forgave me for ruining it for him, either. He began to disappear for days at a time, but always showed back up eventually, never the worse for wear. He might have kept in mind that I was there to save his hide, but you know cats, it's all about them.

Chapter 3

Alex

After Tanya, we were left with just Booty and two rabbits. Every animal we ever had taught us something. These rabbits taught us that people trying to unload small animals will look you in the eye and lie right to your face—about anything and everything. I would find myself copying their reprehensible behavior less than a year later.

A friend had a rabbit that had a litter, or whatever you call a bunch of baby bunnies. I brought the children over to see them. I was warned by Rich ahead of time not to bring one home. I didn't. I brought two. The kids were at a particularly cute age, and the bunnies looked like they had just hopped off an Easter card. I knew I was pushing it with two, and I did ask if I could just take one. I was told that one rabbit would be lonely. That was just the beginning of the lies.

I would find out later that two rabbits of the same gender will fight when they mature. I didn't know that then. Anyway, each child wanted his or her own rabbit. Different genders just make more rabbits, so my main concern was that whatever baby bunnies they picked out were of the same sex.

I guess I could have figured out which one that was had I looked, but I never did. I didn't do it for kittens, either. I mean, I knew what to look for, of course, and in dogs it is pretty obvious, but in the smaller, furrier animals you really have to *look*. It struck me as rather rude. So I never did it, still haven't, and it still strikes me as rude.

However, as Bryan and Andrea jumped from one bunny to the next, my friend would pop it upside down and declare it a male. That was amazing—all those bunnies and not a female in the bunch. Bryan's rabbit was gray and white and named Benjamin Bunny. Andrea's rabbit was all white and named Peter Rabbit. I put them in the back of my car, the first brand-new car we would ever own. It was a bright-red Pacer. No wonder the rabbit owner saw me as an easy mark

As I pulled into the driveway, I saw our neighbor from across the street raking his lawn. "Hey, Harold," I shouted, "come see what I got the kids."

He crossed the street and glanced into the hatchback portion of the car. "Rich is going to kill you."

"I know." I was now getting a little nervous. "You want them?"

He laughed and went back to raking his yard. The kids ran into the house, without the bunnies, and never showed the slightest interest in them again. Okay, that may be an exaggeration, but any future interest would indeed be slight.

When Rich got home, he went about constructing proper housing for the new family members. He made a large cage out of wood and wire and a snug little hutch made of wood. He attached the entire thing to the inside of the stockade fence. He didn't yell or chastise me. He didn't say anything. I think he knew all along I would probably drag them home, but there was a whole lot of quiet in our house that night. I hate that. I take it as a rebuke, which of course it was. The only thing he asked was if the rabbits were of the same sex so he would know if he had to make one cage or two.

I assured him they were both male. I mean, one was named Benjamin, and one was named Peter. Of course they were male. Of course my children had named them.

That spring we were up to our knees in baby bunnies. Well, maybe not that many, but quite a few for two males to produce. Andrea once locked her bunny in her lunch box. Bryan told on her, and I dismissed his accusation, asserting the bunny was much too big to fit.

"I folded him," said my small daughter.

I raced downstairs to the playroom, and indeed, Peter was in her lunch box. Folding him did not seem to have harmed him at all, except that, months later, he became the proud mother of six baby bunnies. I don't think the lunch box had anything to do with it, but I refuse to rule it out. Rich immediately put a divider in the pen and made a second hutch for the other side. We were amazed to watch the new mom.

It was spring and it was warm. The babies were born with no fur and their eyes shut. Kind of creepy looking, really. Peter would pluck fur from her body to cover the babies at night and then remove it during the day so they wouldn't get too warm.

"Wow," Rich said, "I guess we're lucky she's such a good mom." We wouldn't have known what to do. But we both admitted it was pretty fascinating. The children were inside watching cartoons. Peter may have been a good mother, but she sure wasn't great.

All of the babies looked different, had different colors and markings. And one little baby kept getting thrown out of the nest. I called my friend and was told if something were wrong with the baby, the mother wouldn't feed it. I tried putting a plastic bag on my hand (to eliminate any telltale human odor) and mixing them up, but the mom always recognized this particular little soul and booted him out. I tried feeding him with a doll's bottle and an eyedropper, but it didn't work. He was just too little. He needed his mom to feed him, and nothing we could do could make that happen.

I never thought of rabbits as vocal. I mean, we had these two for over six months before the blessed event and never heard a peep out of them. We never even knew more bunnies were on the way until they showed up. In our defense, they were pretty fluffy, not a bad way to disguise a pregnancy. But this little baby rabbit would cry out; he was hungry. I can't describe the pathetic noise he made, but I could hear it anywhere, particularly in my sleep.

"He's starving to death," I said.

"I know," Rich said.

"He's suffering, poor little thing."

"I know."

"You should kill him."

"*What?*"

"So he won't have to suffer anymore. He's going to die anyway. Just put the poor little guy out of his misery." I didn't add, *And me out of mine.*

"Why me? Why don't you do it?"

"I don't know how, and anyway, you're the man."

"So?"

"You were in the Marines; they taught you how to kill."

"Not bunnies."

By the time we finished this argument, never coming to a conclusion anyway, the bunny had passed away on its own. Its siblings were growing, covered in fur and beginning to look like Easter card material, just the same as their parents. Now we had to find homes for them. This is when I sunk to my friend's level, telling people I knew what gender they were (and, no, I never looked), how to take care of them, how lonely they would be if they only took one...Finding homes for them is hard, which is what reduces you to this unfortunate state.

I found myself approaching the parents of my children's friends. I tried to choose parents that were alone and attending one of their children's functions. I was afraid if both parents were present they might bring common sense into the equation. That was not the problem with one dad.

"Hi." I tried a friendly and not conniving smile.,

"Hi."

"Do you like rabbits?"

"Yeah, they're delicious, why?"

"Never mind."

Eventually, all the little babies were placed in new homes and this small drama ended. Just in time for the next one. Booty had disappeared again, this time for an unusually protracted period of time. Personally, I thought he had just found a home with an accommodating dog and was back to his old tricks. Fate wasn't going to be that kind.

One morning, I heard a rustling in the bushes, and there he was. He didn't appear to be hurt, and shades of Pinky crossed my mind. I really thought he would be fine. The kids hadn't gone to school yet, and we all gathered around patting him and welcoming him home. And then he screamed. Obviously, all was not well, but I didn't know what the heck the problem was or how serious it was. I put out food and milk for him, and he ate like he hadn't eaten in a week, which he probably hadn't.

Then he went to jump on the couch, and he screamed (that's really the only word for it) again. It was his right front leg. He couldn't put any weight on it at all. I guessed it was probably broken. I told the kids that he would be fine and that I would take him to the veterinarian after they left for school. I seriously pictured bringing him home with a little cast on his front leg.

I called the office, and they told me I could bring him in. I still had the Pacer, and it had been sitting in the sun all morning. When we bought it, it was the first year they came out, and it didn't come with air-conditioning. All that glass in the huge windows really caused that little bubble of a car to heat up. I wrapped the cat in a towel and put him on my lap in the car. We now had a veterinarian's office in our town, only about five minutes from where we lived. As it turned out, that was not going to be close enough.

The poor cat threw up everything it had eaten since he got home. It missed me, at least mostly, but the front seats of the car were pretty bad. When I carried him into the office, I was told there were several other people in front of me and we would have to wait. I couldn't believe it. I don't mind waiting my turn—I expect to—but the cat was in pain, and I told the receptionist that. Some of the puppies were just there for their shots.

She looked at me and said, quite seriously, "Cats don't really feel pain, not like people."

She was an idiot. But pointing that out wasn't going to get Booty seen any sooner. So we had to wait. The poor cat in pain and my car baking in the sun, getting ranker by the moment.

When we finally got to see the doctor, he told me the cat had obviously been hit by a car. I was amazed; he didn't seem to have a mark on him. What I was shown, and hadn't noticed, were all of his claws were either missing or badly torn up. I was told this often happens when a cat is struck by a moving vehicle; they automatically try to dig their claws in. I was also told they would have to take X-rays and would call me when they had the results.

When I opened the door to my car, I almost passed out. The smell was unbelievable. When I got home, I got busy with soap and water and disinfectant and brushes. I had just finished when the call came in to return to the office. They had the results of the X-rays.

It was pretty amazing, but the only injury Booty sustained was to his leg. But what an injury it was. They had counted at least nineteen breaks. They said they could operate, but couldn't guarantee they could wire all the pieces back together again. If they couldn't, they informed me cheerfully they could just amputate the leg. *Some cats do very well on three legs*, I was told. At any rate, they would try to save it. Then they told me how much this surgery would cost. I was dizzy for the second time that day.

I couldn't tell you the price (I don't remember), but if you adjusted it for inflation, I think it would be around the national debt. I already owed them for the X-rays and examination. That was going to come out of that week's grocery and mortgage money. All I would get out of it was a dead cat. I told them to just put him to sleep. Of course I would have to pay for that, too. Please know I didn't do this lightly. I really did like this cat—okay, maybe even loved him—and he deserved better. By this time, however, he was getting on in years, and he only lived with us part time. Also, I couldn't picture this former conman hobbling around on three legs. That's assuming he survived the surgery and they couldn't wire him back together. There wasn't any extra money to go around, so it seemed like a no-brainer to me. The hospital workers looked shocked. They suggested I discuss it with my husband or perhaps my children.

Okay, even I'm not that mean. I made the decision, paid what was owed, and asked to see the cat one last time. That was a mistake. When he saw me, he got up, still groggy from the X-rays, but licked my hand in expectation of going home. It broke my heart, but it wouldn't be the first or the last time I would have my heart broken by an animal.

Then I got to tell the kids. They were older now, and I explained that the cat had been hit by a car and was not going to make it. My son stoically went to his room. Annie stared at me.

"What?" I said.

"Couldn't the veterinarian do anything? You said they would help him."

I explained about the surgery, omitting the cost, and told her it probably wouldn't work anyway.

"It was the money, wasn't it?" (How did she know? I never told her the cost.)

"No, I didn't want him to suffer."

"And it was about the money."

"No, I didn't want him to have just three legs."

"And it was about the money."

"A little bit."

Couldn't fool her then; can't fool her now.

Now we were down to just two rabbits. The life expectancy for a rabbit of this type was about three to five years. That was about as long as Peter lived. Benjamin lived practically forever. I know Bryan was in early grade school when we got him and was almost ready for college by the time his rabbit passed away. We had already gotten a replacement rabbit for Andrea, and it also passed away around the appointed time, but Benjamin soldiered on. I'm sure he could have made the *Guinness Book of World Records*, but I have no proof. You never think of things like then when they are happening.

Even before Benjamin finally gave up the ghost, so to speak, in our minds we were running dangerously low on pets. Since we had gotten Tanya for Bryan, and his interests had now turned to girls, we thought we should get a dog for Andrea. I had forgotten about the difference in the ages that boys and girls mature. Seems my daughter's interest had also turned to the opposite sex. We didn't recognize that fact until after we obtained the dog, but honestly, we probably would have gotten him anyway.

We got another white German shepherd, this one a male. He was much younger than Tanya when we got him, probably about eight or nine weeks old. He looked like a snowball with raisins for his eyes and nose. We named him Alex. Who could possibly resist this adorable ball of fluff? Our hormone-crazed offspring, that's who.

I remember having friends over for coffee and Alex playing in the backyard. He began to climb the four steps to the deck. He had never accomplished this before. The four of us noticed his efforts as we sat at the kitchen table with our coffee. We all went to the glass door and watched as, first, one tiny front paw and then the other popped over the first stair followed by a teeny black nose, his back legs scrambling like mad to push himself up. We began to cheer him on. No professional football team has ever been blessed with such enthusiastic fans. He triumphantly made it to the deck, a feat we place in importance right up there with the first moon walk.

Alex would grow into a beautiful dog. He was really our dog since the kids only paid passing attention to him. Actually, since we had two teenagers at that point, so did we. Luckily, he was a good dog and low maintenance, so he didn't require all that much.

Benjamin was still with us at this time, and we used to let him out to run around the yard if we were out there with Alex. Alex never bothered him in his cage, and once when a stray dog got into our yard and headed directly for the rabbit cage, Alex drove him off.

We didn't think he would ever hurt the rabbit, but to be on the safe side, if Benjamin hopped even near Alex, we would give Alex a firm "let him be" command. Alex never made a move toward him. Benjamin picked up on this (I know he was just a dumb bunny, supposedly, but I've always thought all animals and little children are far smarter than given credit for) and hopped toward the dog. If Alex was lying down, he would hop right over to him. Alex, afraid of getting into trouble—as you know, dogs are born feeling guilty—would get up and move.

This progressed to the point that no matter where the dog settled, along came Benjamin, at which time the dog would run away. In no time at all, you could come to our house and watch a small gray-and-white bunny chase a hundred-pound dog all over the place. I suspect they both enjoyed this type of play. I was just concerned that Benjamin thought of himself as some sort of super rabbit and might try this on a strange dog. Luckily, the situation never presented itself.

The only other incident I remember with Alex was on a very cold, snowy day when he got out of the yard. He was probably suffering at least a little from lack of attention, and he took off but didn't really run away. We could tell because he would stay just far enough ahead of us so we couldn't catch him and kept glancing back to make sure we were there.

We chased him all over town, at one point even crossing a frozen pond. Rich went home to get the car. A full-grown shepherd in peak condition can cover a lot of ground, even if he did pause occasionally for his owners to almost catch up.

He darted into a neighborhood that we didn't know. Rich had parked the car at the end of the street, and we were close behind him. As we turned the corner into a stranger's yard, we heard a tremendous bark. Alex was no slouch when it came to barking, but this one seemed even louder and deeper.

Rich was ahead of me and screeched to a stop.

"That dog is even bigger than Alex! That dog is huge!"

When I came to a breathless stop, I looked up at the largest black-and-white Great Dane I have ever seen in my life. He and Alex were making friends, and that gave us the opportunity to slip over to Alex and place a leash on his collar. Luckily, the Great Dane seemed friendly enough.

At that point, a man walked out of the house, the one attached to the property we were standing on.

"Is that your dog?" He was rather belligerent about it.

I couldn't help thinking if we were actually stealing dogs, then we certainly weren't showing any talent for it.

"Yes," I muttered, "he got out of the yard and—"

"Why don't you people take the time to teach your dogs to stay in their own yard like I do?"

"Well, yes, of course we should." We both apologized profusely as we made our way back to the car.

There was only one answer to his question: We were bad pet owners. You would think we would be better with all the practice we had. It wasn't until we were backing the car around when I noticed a huge chain, like the type you use to secure a boat or small aircraft, running from the Great Dane's collar, then being partially obscured by snow, but emerging on the side of the doghouse, where it was secured by a large metal bolt. Really wish I had seen that earlier. This whole walk of shame thing was getting old.

Chapter 4

Max

"You can take pets on the beach after September fifteenth," said Rich as he read the posted signs. "I didn't know that."

We were strolling hand and hand along an almost deserted stretch of Rhode Island coastline on a chilly fall day.

"I didn't know that, either," I replied. "Thinking about Maxie?"

"Yeah," he admitted, "I'll bet he would have loved the waves."

Such was the irony of a dog that could not swim but loved the water. He loved kiddie pools, sprinklers (taking him for a walk in the summer was an adventure as he lunged at and sometimes retrieved other people's water devices), ponds, and streams. Because of his obvious joy in the water, we took it upon ourselves to teach him how to swim.

I swear it wasn't until many, many years after his passing that we were to learn from some educational TV show that bullmastiffs, which was what Max was, cannot swim. Their body mass is too dense. We had never heard of a dog that couldn't swim, so there was nothing to deter us. Certainly not Max. He loved the water, and he loved Rich even more. He cheerfully followed Rich into Tiogue Lake until the water became too deep, at which point he would sink like a stone, fully confident that we would rescue him. And of course we did, pulling him up from the bottom with his eyes and nose streaming water. That was pretty much how that summer went. The lake was right down the street from us, and neither we nor the dog ever got a clue. None of us lost any eagerness for trying, either. You would have thought Max might, being the drownee and all, but he took to every trip with unabashed enthusiasm. They all went the same exact same way. Dogs are really good sports.

After the loss of Alex, who had pretty much lived a full, if uneventful life, we were without pets. For some reason, no new cats had emerged. The children were grown and gone as well. We talked about getting another dog, but we were both working full time at this point, and after our lovely German shepherds, wouldn't any other dog pale in comparison?

Still, the nagging feeling of something missing and the flash of loneliness that can come from entering an empty house started to take its toll. What if we got a different breed, one that wasn't as active as a working dog? I spoke to our veterinarian, and he suggested a bullmastiff. I got out the encyclopedia and started to read. Bullmastiffs were a huge, approximately 150 pounds and up. They have low energy and are basically born retired. They love their creature comforts, such as air conditioners and fireplaces.

They are even suggested for apartment living. Bullmastiffs, I told Rich, was the breed for us.

There was only one negative. These dogs were, well, kind of ugly. Rich asked what I meant by ugly, and I pulled out a picture of a huge, heavily jowled, muscular dog with a pushed-in face and an amazingly depressed expression.

"Well, what do you want—a dog or a prom date?" he cracked.

That was how we found ourselves knee-deep in a litter of floppy-eared puppies. As Rich moved from puppy to puppy, he found himself hampered by a red brindle male that was hanging on to his boot laces with grim determination. When Rich whistled to the pup, its gaze moved slowly from Rich's boots up to the top of his head, at which point the puppy promptly fell over backward. As he regained his footing, his shining eyes fixed directly on Rich's face. We had ourselves a new dog.

We would learn—the hard way, the way we learn almost everything—that, as a breed, Bullmastiffs are giant, people-loving dogs. Obedience, however, is not their strong suit. This fact was clearly driven home to me when, in the middle of the shortest lesson, or even a mild scolding, Max would simply get up and wander away. Some people take this as a sign of not being very bright. Don't believe it. Max did what he wanted when he wanted more often than any other dog we had up to that point.

I will admit to a lack of focus when he was a puppy, but really nothing much bothered him. We made adjustments for him rather than the other way around.

Housebreaking was, to be kind, a challenge. I'll spare you the details. When Max grew too big to be confined to a crate, we bought a baby gate to put at the top of the stairs. That way he had the entire lower floor, scattered with dog toys, to romp and play in. This arrangement worked for a short time, until one day when I failed to close the gate securely.

I came home to a house filled with overturned plants, blankets pulled from beds, and towels ripped from the bathroom. The basket of fresh fruit I always left out on the coffee table was gone and the fruit half eaten. Actually, except for the handle, so was the basket. Maxie was exhausted; he had a busy day. He lay snoring in a pile of bedding on the floor. Yes, he snored. He also drooled, but just a little. The next day, I was sure to secure that gate. When I arrived home from work, Max was upstairs, having consumed a new basket of fruit, the basket, and most of the baby gate.

This was just puppy stuff; however, it was magnified by his size. I would look at him lying on the kitchen floor and I could have sworn I could see him growing. Either that or the walls were closing in. Like a child, he outgrew this destructive phase all on his own, thank goodness. But he would forever remain unique. One of the great eye-rollers of all time, he employed this tactic whenever he was told to do something he didn't want to do. These dogs have incredibly expressive faces. He would plop his head down between massive front paws and emit a heavy sigh while gazing at you from beneath arched eyebrows. This underlined his impatience with a breed of owner he had obviously determined to be not too bright.

Although people were understandably intimidated by Max's size, his disposition won him some admirers.

The man from the water company was supposed to come move our meter. Apparently, after doing a drive-by and seeing Max in the backyard, they called to ask me to be home so I could take the dog in while they tended to the meter. They couldn't tell me the exact time, so I missed a day of work. When the meter reader showed up, Max was hanging his head over the fence in curiosity. It was a four-foot stockade fence, to give you an idea of his size. I immediately went outside to take him in.

This was apparently a different meter reader, and he said, "Could you leave him outside? I've never seen a dog like this before."

Of course I agreed. Max was no threat, and since the meter reader was reaching over the fence to scratch his ears, I couldn't discern a problem for anyone. He left the dog to go around the corner of the house to the meter, but before he got to the meter, and before I had a chance to go in the house, he came back.

"What kind of dog is that? Is it a purebred?" This while resuming ear scratching.

I told him the breed and that it was a purebred, but hardly rare and not all that expensive. You just didn't see many of them because they are so large that a lot of people think it costs a fortune to feed them. Actually, Max ate less than our German shepherds. He expended a lot less energy.

"I used to have a dog, but had to get rid of it because I lived in an apartment."

I expressed my condolences.

He left to move the meter again, but he came back. Again. "I love his face; he's so expressive. You know, if Jim Hensen made a Muppet dog, it would look just like this one."

I agreed. He left to finish the job, and I pondered my lost day of pay.

When he returned, he said, "You know, I have a house now. There is no reason in the world that I couldn't have another dog. Dammit, I'm getting a dog. And I want one just like this one. "

I gave him the name of the breeder we bought Max from and wished him well. If it worked out for him and the dog, I guess it was worth the day's pay.

Many giant breeds don't live that long, but Max would succumb to bone cancer at the tender age of two and a half. Maxie had been such a wonderful and unexpected surprise. He had added a new dimension to our lives, and we were still learning about him and what he could teach us.

We never expected much from him. We didn't get him to be a watchdog, or a show dog, or to breed. I guess we just needed to fill that void in our lives. The irony was that he gave us so very much more. During a difficult time in our lives, he was not only there, but he made us laugh. He understood us and what we needed more than we had any right to expect.

What do you do when you're nowhere near finished, barely begun, actually, and the end comes anyway?

Chapter 5

Luther and All Things Wild and Wooly

With our children grown and both of us working full time, we began to investigate the option of moving closer to Rich's work. This would save time on his commute and give us more time with each other. We also decided to try another bullmastiff. We went to look at a puppy, a little female, but as I watched her rocket around the house and thought of the hours I was working, it seemed a bit much. The breeder told me their stud dog was also for sale. They were getting out of the business. His name was Luther, and he was about five years old. His mate, also for sale, was named Cricket.

We went to a pen in the backyard and saw them. They were both spectacular looking. However, Cricket came over to see us and then wandered away, apparently bored with both of us. Luther stayed by the fence, wagging his tail tentatively and looking at us in what I took to be a wistful manner. He was a tan dog with a dark muzzle and ears, a real good-looking guy. We knew we were going to take one of them; we just didn't know which one.

On the way home, we stopped at a restaurant and discussed it. We actually considered taking them both. That's how much we had learned. By this time, Rich was driving a truck, but I had a Saturn. Although we both worked, I usually ended up taking the animals wherever they had to go. It occurred to us that two giant bullmastiffs might not even fit in a Saturn. This was one of the few times when common sense actually entered into the situation.

The problem was we didn't know which one to take. We both had a preference, but we didn't know which one that was for the other person. I suggested we write the name of the preferred dog on a piece of paper and then exchange it. It worked, we both saw something special in Luther.

The owner also told us he didn't drool. All bullmastiffs drool, at least a little, much like a St. Bernard; they have the same shape head and jaw. It didn't bother me because Max had actually drooled very little and I was already used to people who were lying about animals to make a sale.

Surprisingly, this woman had not. Since Luther had been used for breeding, he had never been neutered. As soon as we got him home, we made arrangements to have that taken care of. I had noticed Luther really didn't drool, not at all, but I didn't know why.

When we brought him in for his surgery, the veterinarian picked up on it as well. "Wow, he doesn't drool. How come?"

If he didn't know, I sure didn't. He started to exam Luther's jaw and told us he had a tighter lip than most bullmastiffs, which was why he didn't drool. He also remarked on the good looks and the level temperament of the dog in general. Most of the breed tends to be pretty placid, but he told us that the lack of drooling made Luther the perfect specimen. He suggested, instead of neutering him, we should consider breeding him.

Okay, I still had the bunny situation firmly imbedded in my mind. I never intended to breed anything else, and I never have. Lord knows I hadn't intended on breeding the rabbits. The surgery went on as planned.

Luther sailed through the surgery, and although he had been used for breeding, he never showed any interest in it again. I guess once you do it for a living, it kind of takes the thrill out of it. I'm just guessing here.

Max certainly had been interested even though we had him fixed at a very early age. Once, when we had company, he dragged a couple of blankets into the middle of the living room. Then he proceeded to push them around and lump them together. We all thought he was making a nest to be comfortable in and thought it was rather charming. When he was done, however, he didn't see it as a nest; he saw it as the love of his life and commenced to lavish it with "affection." He may have been comfortable, but the rest of us sure weren't.

Luther was only with us a short time when we found a piece of land on which to build a house. It was considerably closer to Rich's work, and that meant reducing the commute time by over an hour each way. This land was what I thought of as country, and we had to buy a minimum of five acres. Although it was a heavily forested lot, I still thought of it as farm country. It was in the farthest northwest corner of Rhode Island. If you walked a quarter of a mile north down our street, you were in Massachusetts. Two miles to the west and you were in Connecticut.

Also, if you approached from the Massachusetts side, there was a sign that said Douglas State Forest. So I wasn't going to be living in farm country; I was going to be living in the woods. I didn't figure that out for a while, since I was always approaching from the Rhode Island side, and that side had no sign. You kind of have to spell things out for me.

I remember the day the environment of our location became clearer to me. I was working the night shift as a life insurance underwriter, and my hours were from 1:00 p.m. to 9:00 p.m., which got me home around 10:00 p.m. Usually, I would walk Luther around our property when I got home so he could "do his business" and be in for the night.

Luther was such a good soul. I never had to put a leash on him, and while we walked, he would discretely disappear into the brush for a few minutes and then reappear, all set to go in and go to bed. He didn't like being watched, and I wasn't crazy about watching, so it worked out well for both of us. Also, since it was our property and he chose secluded areas, I didn't have to clean up after him, either. Does it get any better than that?

Not long after we began these walks, I was stopped in my tracks by something moving through the trees. It wasn't a deer; it was the wrong shape and didn't bolt away at our approach. When it turned to look at me, it was built like a very large teddy bear. I honestly didn't get much of a look; besides the darkness, I wasn't wearing my glasses. Whatever it was, I was stunned and looked around for Luther to try and gage his reaction. He was nowhere in sight. I never even heard him leave. When I turned back, whatever it had been was gone. I walked back to the house alone. Luther was waiting at the garage door to be let in. Okay, he lost some loyalty points.

When I went into the house, I said to Rich, "I think we have a bear in the backyard."

"Don't be silly, there are no bears here."

"I didn't think so, either, but I saw something." Since it had never occurred to me that we might have bears (I was still thinking farm country, with cows and sheep and stuff like that), I was pretty confident that it wasn't my imagination.

"It was probably just a moth."

A *moth? A MOTH?*

"If it's a bear, I'll deal with it; if there are moths that big, I'm out of here."

The next night when I got home, Rich was sitting in the kitchen with Luther. He had already taken him for his walk. He looked kind of confused, sitting there turning his flashlight on and off.

"You saw it, too, didn't you? You saw a bear."

"I don't know what I saw," he said hesitantly and then added, "but I'm getting a bigger flashlight."

After checking for tracks in the daylight and a few more sightings, we were able to determine we did indeed have a small black bear living in the woods behind our house. He turned out to be a fine neighbor, never coming too close to the house, remaining quiet, and never bothering anyone. And we didn't bother him. When the property around us was sold and developed, he moved away.

I guess it was too crowded for him, but wherever he is, we wish him well. It is kind of cool to live comfortably with wild creatures. We miss him. We also have a ton of deer, rabbits, coyotes, foxes, and our house became a feeding station for hummingbirds. I loved the tiny little birds and had seen a dead one in our garage. Hummingbirds are attracted to the color red, and our automatic garage door openers had large red tags on them. We suspected one had flown in and been trapped, unknowingly, by us and eventually died.

Since we knew they were in the area, it seemed reasonable to put up a hummingbird feeder in the hopes of attracting them. I bought one from the Audubon Society that was made of clear plastic with red plastic flowers over the feeding holes. It came with instructions on how to attract hummingbirds. This included tying a red ribbon to the feeder, which side of the house to place it on, and things of that nature.

I popped it out of the box, disregarded everything in the pamphlet (one of the few instructional guides I've ever read), and placed the feeder on the window in the breakfast nook. It fastened with suction cups, and if the birds should actually show up, we could watch them while we ate or sat at the kitchen table drinking coffee. The booklet warned it could take weeks or even months to attract a bird. Also, I wasn't paying any attention to their helpful hints, so I wasn't sure if we would see one at all.

I filled the feeder with sugar water and attached it to the middle window of a three-sectioned bay window that was in the kitchen, facing the back of the house. When I turned away from the window, I thought a saw a flash of something out of the corner of my eye. Like the first bear sighting, I wasn't sure I saw anything at all. I stood still for a moment and watched.

A few minutes later, a hummingbird appeared and hovered over the feeder. He dipped his beak to drink, but didn't land. A few minutes after that, another hummingbird arrived; this one landed and drank deeply. I don't know how many birds were using the feeder because they move so fast and are so small. I know we had enough so that we bought a second feeder, and soon that one was full of birds as well. I'm not much of a cook, but I must mix up some dynamite sugar water.

We kept the feeders going for a few years, and then one broke. I didn't replace it. Let's face it, the novelty had worn off. I kept filling the remaining feeder every three to five days. A couple of years later, that one broke too. I decided not to replace it. There were plenty of flowers they could drink from, and it was beginning to seem like a chore.

I usually put the feeder out at the beginning of April and took it in sometime in September. The year I decided not to replace it, I heard a humming coming from the back of the house. I never remembered hearing them from inside before, but I guess I hadn't upset them before, either. I looked at the window, and sure enough, there was a hummingbird hovering where the feeder was usually placed. They don't just fly by; they can hover like a helicopter, sometimes moving a little up and down or side to side, but never leaving the spot completely. And that's what he did, hovered and stared and, in my mind, judged me. I suspected I wasn't coming off too well.

I figured once he realized there was no free lunch coming, he would move on. He didn't. I called the Audubon Society and asked the life span of an average Ruby-throated Hummingbird. I was told the average was three to five years, but they could easily live to fourteen. The life span of Benjamin Bunny flashed through my mind. I then asked if they would return to the same feeding spot they were used to after migrating south for the winter. I was told that it would most likely become a permanent stop for them every year. Damn. I grabbed my car keys and walked out the door. Rich asked where I was going.

"To buy another bird feeder."

"I thought you weren't going to do that anymore."

"Tell them."

A new feeder was attached to the window, and one remains there to this day. Dogs aren't the only ones born feeling guilty.

Chapter 6
Lil' Bitty

I wasn't looking for a cat when Lil' Bitty came into our lives. We had Luther and all of the wildlife, so I felt we had enough animals to keep us going. Even the deer had become pushy. They ate all of our shrubs, which we replaced every year until we learned to cover them with burlap in the winter, and most of our flowers. Our house was a Garrison Colonial with a farmer's porch wrapped around the front. The deer became so bold that, one day, when I was setting the dining room table, I felt something looking at me. I glanced up at the front window, and a lovely doe was peering in. My sudden movement startled her. She turned and leapt over the railing and off the porch. Apparently, they don't need a running start to jump.

In all fairness to the deer, we loved seeing them, especially the little ones in the spring. We purposely planted flowers that attracted them. After hunting season ended, when the winters got really cruel, we would put out corn for them to eat. I don't know why, but this is against the law. I just ask you not turn us in. One year, during a particularly brutal winter, we read about deer being found dead with rocks and dirt in their stomachs, trying to ease the hunger pains. That did it, and the corn feeding began. One night, when I got home late, I went to the garage and got a big bucket of corn. It was pitch black out, and Rich offered to come with me. I declined, as I was only going to be a minute. The ground was covered with about a foot of snow, and frozen sleet had covered the snow. There was a coating of ice on the trees, so the deer couldn't even eat the bark. There had not been any melting in days. I started to empty the corn onto the frozen ground.

As soon as the first kernel struck the ground, something in the woods started to move. I knew it was just a deer, so I continued. It was like the entire forest came alive. Although I couldn't make out distinct shapes, I could see shadows moving toward me from all sides. I was completely surrounded. For some reason, Stephen King novels flashed through my mind. I dumped the corn in a pile and ran for the house. After that, we greatly increased our supply of corn and tried to get it dumped before it got dark.

But I digress. I was explaining how we obtained Lil' Bitty. I was working part time at as a receptionist for an independent insurance agent. His wife was the office manager and an animal lover, as was everyone who worked there. The office was more like a house, with a yard, and we used to watch a pair of feral cats in the back. The wife fed them regularly, but they certainly weren't tame. While I was working there, we saw an adorable litter of various-colored kittens emerge and begin to grow. They were pretty small but large enough to be taken from their mom, assuming anyone could.

At about this time, the office manager asked me if I could do a report on the computer. I was fairly competent on the computer, but the program she wanted me to use was Excel. I had learned Excel at another job and hated it. I hadn't found it user friendly at all. I had forgotten how to use it anyway. I told her that, and she graciously offered to teach it to me. I had no interest in learning it again, but I really couldn't say that. While this was going on, she became more and more obsessed with finding homes for the kittens. She asked me whether I would take one home if she could catch them.

I had been watching them right along with her. Although they would come eat the food that was left out, the kittens were as fast as quicksilver. It appeared that catching one or all of them was as likely as snagging a shooting star. I quickly agreed. I reasoned that while she was distracted trying to catch the impossible, I would do the report in good old-fashioned Microsoft Word.

As soon as we reached the agreement, she went into the basement and came up with a Havahart raccoon trap. I honestly didn't see that coming. She placed it outside and, within minutes, came in with my new cat. And I had to learn Excel. Again. Sometimes life isn't all that fair.

The upside was I really fell in love with this new little guy. He was so small and timid. I swear instead of "meow" he said "Mama." Sometimes when I sat on the porch with him, he would dart into the woods in front of the house. Within minutes, he would become frightened and start calling out. I tried calling his name, but got no response. Then I tried meowing back, and I heard a rustle and an answering meow. I kept it up until he followed my voice back to the house. This became a regular game for us. As long as he didn't stray too far, I enjoyed it. For some reason, no one suggested institutionalizing the crazy lady who sat on her front steps meowing like a cat. Sometimes you catch a break.

I wasn't at all concerned about introducing the kitten to Luther. The thing you have to understand about Luther is that he probably had stronger maternal instincts than I did.

Shortly after we got him, we began to augment his usual toys with stuffed animals, the kind that squeak. The first one was a dog toy that we called Luther's "mousy," because, obviously, it looked like a mouse, but was much larger, and if you squeezed it, it squeaked. Luther adored it; he licked it, sniffed it, and carried it around all day. At night, before he went to bed, he would gently place it in his dog bed. He slept on the floor. It eventually got so rank I decided to replace it. I got an identical one, placed it in his dog bed when he wasn't looking, and tossed the original in the trash. Wouldn't it be lovely if life were that simple?

Luther never rooted around in the trash; we didn't have to worry about that. The very next day, however, although he started carry around the new toy, he walked around the house in an agitated fashion, looking everywhere. Our kitchen trash had a pedal you were supposed to step on to open the cover. Rich and I never did; we just lifted the cover and tossed things in. For some reason, on this day, Luther opened the trash. Yes, he stepped on the pedal (he hadn't learned that from us) and peered inside. Sitting right on top was *his* mousy. He retrieved it with a look of betrayal that went right to my soul. It now smelled even worse.

Rich took him for a car ride, and I tossed it in the washer and dryer and prayed it would survive. It did, but I didn't know if he would accept it as the same mouse since it now smelled almost as good as the new one.

By the time my guys returned, the cleaned mouse was on Luther's rug, along with the new one. That solved the problem. Somehow, and I don't pretend to know how, he knew it was the original. He now had two mice, so to speak. His love for them knew no bounds.

When friends saw his interaction with his mice, they started to bring him all sorts of stuffed toys, and he loved them all. And nary a one came to any harm under his care. So when I brought home Lil' Bitty, his eyes lit up. Another baby for him to care for. I know he was male, and I don't understand it, either. When I put the kitten on the floor, Luther gently approached him, tail wagging slowly. This little scrap of a kitten took in the moving mountain of a dog and immediately swatted him across the nose. Luther didn't care. Lil' Bitty could be the boss, which he was, but now Luther had a living, breathing little being to take care of, and he did.

They became inseparable buddies. When we occasionally boarded them, I asked the owner to put Lil' Bitty with Luther if Luther seemed despondent. She looked skeptical, but agreed. I don't know if Luther ever seemed unhappy. I do know this woman felt compelled to give it a try. (I don't blame her; I would've, too.) When we returned, she told us, with great relish, how she would tell the kennel workers that they had to take his kitten with him when they took Luther outside. They all thought she was playing some kind of joke on them. Apparently, Luther and Bitty turned them all into believers.

We had a chain-link fence around the deck, and we used that enclosure to take the kitten out to play. We had originally put it up for Luther, but he didn't need physical boundaries to keep him home. I had taken Luther for a restroom walk, and when we returned, as we approached the house, we could see Rich playing with the kitten behind the fence. Luther took off like a shot straight for them. Seeing a 150-pound dog in full gallop is pretty impressive and didn't happen that often. Luther never saw the need to move that fast before—except once when he chased a pheasant. The pheasant took flight as soon as he got close. I guess he figured it was a losing proposition. He never bothered again.

When we first brought him to the new house, Rich was concerned Luther might chase the deer and catch one. I didn't know if he would chase one, but I was positive he wouldn't catch it. After all, the deer were built like missiles. Luther was built like a dump truck. In the end, it didn't matter; he declined to even chase them.

But on this day, he never wavered; he was full speed ahead, caution to the wind. Both Rich and I were shocked and didn't know what provoked it. We weren't worried because there was that fence between the dog and cat. When Luther got to the fence, he screeched around the corner to the other side. From the underbrush, out shot a fox, running for his life. It had been edging closer and closer to the kitten. Neither Rich nor I had seen it. The kitten didn't, either, but Luther did. Although I don't know if the fox could have gotten over or under the fence, Luther chased him all the way to the street. He wasn't taking any chances with his kitty. And it cost him and us dearly. When he came back, he was limping.

It was obvious that Luther couldn't put any weight on his left hind leg. He never complained, not a whimper or a whine, but it was clear that he couldn't use that leg. We immediately brought him to the veterinarian. We were told he had blown out his knee or in vet speak "ruptured his anterior cruciate ligament." He would need surgery, and of course, this would require a specialist. The bad news was it would cost between $1,800 and $2,500. The good news was we were at a point in our lives, not always the case, when we had, or could gather, that amount of money.

The really good news was the surgery was successful. We bought a crib mattress and put it in the family room and covered it with a comforter. That way Luther didn't have to climb the stairs (he couldn't anyway) and would still be comfortable. When he first came home, he looked terrible. He was lying on his side on the mattress and seemed out of it. Lil' Bitty curled up under his chin and stayed by his side until his recuperation was complete. That was about eight weeks. The day he came home I was a mess. I crouched down over him to hug his head, and he wagged his tail weakly and raised his head to meet me halfway. After a moment, his head must have been too heavy for him to hold up, and he dropped it down on the mattress. Well, it would have been on the mattress if Bitty hadn't been there, but he was, so it landed square on that tiny cat. Again, nobody made a sound. Bitty wiggled and struggled and, with me holding some of the weight of Luther's head, was able to extricate himself. He didn't leave. He just settled back in and waited for his friend to mend.

And mend Luther did. He had several healthy, happy years after that. Unfortunately, being a giant breed usually guarantees a short life span. That was to be the case with the bullmastiffs we had. Although Luther lived much longer than Max, he, too, would develop bone cancer. It started as a lump on his right front leg, the same as Max. When we first saw it, we knew at heart what it was. But we didn't want to face it. However, we knew we had to take him to the vet, and we did. We also knew the outcome. We were right. I've never hated being right about something so much in my life.

While this was going on, we had begun to take horseback riding lessons. I had always been wild about horses, and whenever we went on vacation, we would look for stables that offered rentals or trail rides. The only place we couldn't find one was Las Vegas. They had a huge phone book, with a large portion of it dedicated to "entertainment"; however, we never found anything involving horses. Thank God.

We saw some of the most beautiful parts of this country from the backs of horses. In my opinion, this is the best way to see it. I particularly remember exploring parts of Arizona and Utah, either with a group, or by ourselves, but always on horses. Since we were now living in the country—okay, the woods—we looked for a stable near the new house and explored the option of riding lessons.

Honestly, we really didn't want lessons. We had been riding for quite a while, although I certainly could use improvement. What we were seeking was the company of horses and other people of a like mind, and we found it. We told the instructor we were not interested in competition or showing horses; we just wanted to have fun with them.

We were lucky enough to find a place that allowed that and other people that wanted the same thing. Basically, we just played games, some that you might see in a rodeo, but at a very basic level. Sometimes we did things you probably wouldn't see anywhere else. During this time, I fell off and was bucked off horses, although that never bothered me much. Both Rich and I had the philosophy, "If you don't want to take the fall, don't get on the horse."

Some landings were harder than others, and sometimes I was able to stay aboard and regain control. Those times I usually regretted it and wished I had just let go at the first buck. I had eaten my share of dirt, and it didn't kill me, but if you stay on a horse that continues to buck, you feel like you have been rear-ended in a car crash. The whiplash is murder, and you really feel it in the following days. That's why in a rodeo, whether it is a horse or a bull, you are only required to stay on the animal for eight seconds to qualify for prize money. Take it from me, eight seconds can turn into a very long time.

However, we need to return to the subject of Lil' Bitty. In case you couldn't tell, I've been stalling. Of all the cats we've had, before and after, this was the one that captured my heart the most. He wasn't allowed alone in the woods, for obvious reasons, so when we took Luther for a walk, he would race around the house, from front to back and side to side, and peer out the windows longingly, following our progress.

Finally, we relented and brought him along. He was full grown by then, not that he ever got much bigger. He could climb trees, though, and of course, he had his posse with him. We must have made quite the sight: Luther in the lead, Rich and me following closely behind, and Lil' Bitty bringing up the rear.

I placed a bell on the collar around Bitty's neck so I could always find him. He had a way of disappearing in the house; the washer, dryer, and dishwasher were all fun games for him. Unfortunately, it would have been horrific if I had turned one of them on with him inside. So before turning anything on, I always did a "cat check" to make sure I knew where he was and wasn't.

Once he had a taste of the outdoors, there was no going back. He loved to play in the woods. We always made sure we were home when he was out and got him back inside before nightfall. He usually stayed near the house; occasionally, he would be lured farther into the woods by a bird, or a bug, or something that only he could see. Just as I started to worry, he would pop up. Thankfully, his black-and-white colors worked against his blending in. Just when my heart started to skip a beat, there would be that little face, reassuringly peeking out at me. This worked for quite a while, but one fall day, he didn't come back. We searched, calling his name, meowing like idiots, and listening hopefully for his bell. Nothing.

In desperation, I called the local dog officer. He said he was getting a tremendous amount of calls about lost cats, as he did every year at this time. He asked for a picture, which I sent him. He warned me about getting my hopes up. He explained that this was the time of year when the foxes and coyotes hunted in earnest, getting ready for the long winter. That whole circle of life thing, I guess. I told him another way people could tell it was our cat was the bell around his neck.

"You put a bell on him and sent [*sent?*] him out into the woods at this time of year? Why didn't you just ring a dinner bell?"

Although I'm sure he didn't mean it that way, I guess not everyone subscribes to the theory of not kicking people when they are down. Despite the nearly miraculous returns of Pinky and Booty, this was entirely different terrain. I felt stupid and guilty. The worst part was that Bitty never did come back, and I know he would if he could. Also, the coyote population had exploded that year, so it was impossible for me to convince myself that Bitty had found a better, smarter owner and was living happily ever after with another family.

We still had Luther, that living, breathing reminder that he was a better caretaker than I was, but the seeds of his demise had already been sown. I should have suspected something when he lost interest in looking for his kitty. He had problems of his own. We just didn't know it at the time.

Chapter 7
Horses, Really?

If I haven't already mentioned it, my husband is skilled at just about everything and can play, at least passably, any sport he chooses. I cannot.

I tried tennis, and after weeks of training, the instructor (who was also a friend) could only say, "You're human—that means you have to be able to learn!"

Maybe, but I had no talent for it nor the desire to put in the effort to become ordinary, even sub-ordinary. Well, you get my drift. The one thing I can do is ride a horse. Not necessarily well. I'll refer you to the prior information about getting tossed on my head. Once I even cleverly broke my fall with my face. Nothing got broken, but gravel burn on your face takes some explaining. However, the passion I lacked for other sports was definitely there for this one. I fell in love with horses when I was little, like a lot of preteen girls. Since we lived in the East, with a small house and a small yard, horses were out of our financial and practical reach. Or so my parents thought. But at a very young age—I don't remember which one exactly, but I was still in the single digits—I sat down with pencil and paper to figure out a way to afford a horse. I didn't shine in arithmetic, either.

However, what I lacked in ability I more than made up for in perseverance. By my calculations, if my father stopped drinking, his only recreation, and my mother stopped smoking, her favorite recreation, we could afford a horse for me. Oh, also, my sister would have to drop the dancing and swimming lessons. I would also have to give up dancing lessons, but I hated them anyway. The only reason I took them was because my sister wanted to and we only had one car, which my dad drove to work. My mother felt if she was going to drag us both into the city on the bus, it seemed logical that we both take the lessons. She would live to regret that assumption.

My sister turned into a really good dancer. She still is. I was abysmal and still am. I actually wish I could have learned more. Dancing would have come up more often socially than horseback riding. But, again, I didn't have the interest, or any sense of rhythm. I still don't. We had to perform a recital at the end of the year. I learned all the steps, because I had to. There was no way out; trust me, I looked. My sister and I were to do a duet. I wasn't frightened of the stage. I suspect I was too young and probably not that bright. There is considerable evidence for the latter assumption.

Our number started, and my sister launched into the dance routine in time with the music. Not me. I couldn't pick out the beat to save my life anyway. I just rushed through all the steps I had learned and left the stage. My sister and the music were about halfway through the piece. She angrily motioned me back on stage. I didn't go. I mean, what did she want me to do? I'd used up all the steps they taught me. In my mind, I was done. This was many, many decades ago, and she has since forgiven me. I hope.

I digress; let's return to my grand horse acquisition plan. I had the facts the figures and a plan. The only thing I didn't pick up on was the lay of the land. I can honestly say my dad never hit me. My mom did when we were little, but only an occasional mild swat. So I'm really at a loss to explain how I remember presenting my idea and after that…nothing. I don't remember waking up bruised or woozy. I don't think anybody hit me; it would have been out of character for them anyway. It is possible that their reaction was so severe that my mind has just blocked it out all these years. If that's the case, I have no intention of trying to recover that particular memory. Some things are better left alone.

By the time Rich and I started riding at the aforementioned stable, we were already passed our prime, to put it mildly. We were in our fifties, and while we enjoyed riding tremendously, we had no intention of actually owning our own horse. Honest. Horses are very different from dogs and cats, and we had made some fatal (for the animals) mistakes with them. We had no clue about the care and feeding of such large and sometimes intimidating animals. We were perfectly happy to let them be someone else's responsibility.

However (there always seems to be a however with us), the stable we were riding at brought in some new horses over the fall and winter. We weren't privy to the agreement, but rumor had it that these horses would be fed and stabled for free during this time. In return, they could be used for riding lessons for the students. In the spring, their owner would reclaim them. There were about six of them.

I don't think this arrangement worked out very well, because most of the horses were too hyper to be ridden. However, there was this one… She was a beautiful red quarter horse, about six years old. Unfortunately, she had most of the bad habits in the book. She loved to run and, if she could get her head, would bolt uncontrollably at a reckless speed. Even in an enclosed environment, like an indoor arena or an outside ring, where she had to stop or at least turn eventually because of the barriers, she could and would take you on a wild ride that ended when she wanted it to and not before. She was easily spooked or startled, which would also result in her bolting uncontrollably. She also bucked and was almost impossible to handle on the ground.

The girls who worked there told me they were afraid to clean her stall because she struck out at them with her front feet and bared her teeth. She never actually bit anyone. That we knew of.

She was one of those horses with a shady past. She wasn't registered, and no one knew about her prior life, and if they did, they wouldn't talk about it. We would learn there are a lot of horses like that. She was extremely athletic, and although I'm sure she was part quarter horse, she ran like an Arabian. Her neck arched beautifully, her tail flying high behind her like a flag. She had a white stripe down her nose, and although there are a lot of chestnut horses, she was the deepest red I've ever seen. No one knew what her name was or that of any of the other six horses. Because she was such a rich copper color, she was dubbed "Penny."

Someone had trained her well, at some point, and she could do anything that was asked of her, better than the other twenty or so horses that we had been riding. Barrel racing, pole bending, and keyhole (all gymkhana events) were a breeze for her.

One of the girls who worked at the stable, an excellent rider, had ridden Penny when she first arrived. She knew me, knew what I liked, and told me privately that I would love riding Penny. She said she was smooth and fast and loved to run. A zero-to-sixty kind of gal. You never had to ask her to go; you just had to stop holding her back, assuming you could hold her back—not always a given.

Rich was a better rider than I was (of course, what else was new?), and when we showed interest in Penny, the instructor said that Rich could ride her. She was usually lunged before being ridden. For those who don't know (I didn't) lunging consists of attaching a long lead to the horse's halter and encouraging it to run around you in a circle. An overly energetic horse can race around, buck, and hopefully calm down before being ridden. It's supposed to be a way of neutralizing bad behavior or at least tiring out the horse. We didn't really see Penny's behavior as bad. She was young, and the only time she was turned out of her stall was for the one hour a week Rich rode her. Of course she was full of energy and hard to handle. And, besides, we were in love. All three of us.

Every time I saw Rich on Penny, I wanted a turn. I wanted to ride her so badly I could taste it. Yes, if you haven't already figured it out, I am that stupid. After Rich had ridden her for a while, she calmed a little. The entire time, I haunted the instructor to let me ride her. She finally relented, figuring, I guess, if I hadn't sued by then, I probably wouldn't (and I wouldn't), and I had been tossed on my head so many times that who would believe me anyway?

Now, on alternating Saturdays, one or the other of us would ride her. She was getting easier to handle, but still, it was a thrilling, if unpredictable ride. The part we didn't understand was she would start out behaving reasonably, at least for her, but by the end of the hour, she would be pretty much unmanageable. What made this so unusual is that some horses may start out difficult, but then will settle in when they tire. Penny was just the opposite. It didn't make sense then. It would come together much later when we had gone through a lot of time, tears, and thousands of dollars.

The situation might have stayed at the status quo. We didn't like that she was confined so much, but so were the other horses. She wasn't our horse, so what could we do? We just took more lessons so she got more freedom. Unfortunately, spring came, and Penny, along with the other five horses, would be loaded up and leaving.

We asked the owners of the stable where they would be going but only got evasion. Eventually, we were told they would be going to a "camp" where they could be ridden by children. Everyone in our class was stunned. We were all adults and had some really competent riders in our group. Some had been riding their whole lives. Other than Penny, no one could get near these horses. How were they going to put children on them? The rumor—and I have no way of knowing if it had even a scintilla of truth—was that the horses would probably be drugged.

Rich and I fretted that the only way Penny could be drugged enough to be child safe would be if they put her in a coma. Not only were we riding more than once a week, we had taken to showing up just to visit her. Her stall was in the back of a long, dark hall. One day, when we turned the corner and she saw us, she let out a soft nicker.

A nicker is not the sound most people associate with horses. Most people think they neigh or whinny, and they do. That is the most common thing you will hear, and it is fairly loud and identifiable as coming from a horse. The nicker is a much softer call that a mare will use to her foal or a horse will use to another horse that it is closely attached to. It's not so much a calling out; it isn't that loud. It is more like a soft hello to a friend. Sometimes horses will nicker to the person who feeds them, and that makes sense. Occasionally, they will nicker to those who they have bonded with closely.

Well, we weren't feeding Penny, and this soft greeting turned our already melting hearts to goo. Unfortunately, besides her behavioral problems, Penny had been turning up lame. We had some theories about this. We thought, as many people do, that a horse needs to move to stay healthy. In nature, they walk or run for about eighteen hours a day, only sleeping a few hours at a time. This helps their digestion and their legs. We also didn't like the farrier that was shoeing the horses at the stable. His big claim to fame was his ability to do more horses faster and cheaper than anyone else. While that may have been true, I wouldn't pick a cut-rate doctor that was famous for his speed.

So, basically, what we were dealing with was an unsafe, unsound horse that nobody in his or her right mind would buy. So, of course, we did. We paid a fairly high price for her, too. Not that I'm complaining. We went into it with our eyes wide open. It was our hearts that kept tripping us up. And she was now nickering to us on a regular basis.

Once we bought her, we made arrangements to board her at that stable. Although we had five acres, we had a forest, not a farm. Besides, we didn't know how to care for her. We knew what we didn't like and had a few theories picked up over time, but that was about it. So it seemed the sensible thing to do.

We no sooner purchased her than she came up lame again. It is really tough to tell which leg is hurting a horse. They tend to shift their weight to the remaining legs and try to hide any pain. This is a throwback to being a prey animal, but with neophytes like us, it made it difficult. We could tell her gait was off, knew she was in pain, but that was about it. We called the veterinarian used by the stable.

He didn't like Penny, didn't like the way she nervously jumped around while being examined. I was ready to defend her, but there really didn't seem much point. His mind was made up. He said he thought she had an abscess in her left rear leg. He suggested we soak it in warm water a couple of times a day until it burst. Then he charged us a fortune and left.

Penny didn't kick as a rule, but she was in pain, and any horse can kick. If the veterinarian thought she was hard to handle, you can imagine what flashed though our minds. We stood there with a bucket of warm water and watched our dancing horse with her dangerous hind legs.

She was tied, and Rich raised the afflicted leg while I tried to gingerly slide the bucket underneath. She not only kicked the bucket over she kicked it into the next zip code. We tried again, with Rich cooing to her and massaging her leg before trying to pick it up. Same result, although my nerves were more frayed. The third time was the charm, and she settled into the warm water and relaxed.

She never gave us any trouble after that, but nothing ever burst or drained, either. However, the lameness went away. I still have no idea if the soaking had any effect at all. It may have just healed on its own. We'll never know, but some things you have to take on faith. Also, once Penny found out what it was like to soak her foot, she began to look forward to it. I think she was disappointed when we stopped.

The next thing we found out was that horses have to be wormed every six weeks. This involves a smelly paste that is placed in a syringe-like object. Then you hold the horse's head up and insert the nozzle into the corner of the horse's mouth. You keep her head elevated until she swallows. The whole thing takes about five minutes. At least that's the way it should work. The first time we did it, Rich was in charge of the syringe, and my job was to keep Penny's head elevated. Considering I'm five foot two, this was a stretch, literally. Well, I got her head up, Rich squeezed the paste into her mouth, and I kept her head pointing toward the heavens for what we considered the appropriate time. When I let go, she lowered her head, paused to look at us, and then spit the paste on us. She didn't play favorites; she got us both.

We looked at each other, both dripping with this icky, sticky paste, and we looked at the horse, and then we almost fell over laughing. Isn't it lucky we married each other? We would have driven two other people crazy. But we both thought this was hysterical. I believe Penny did, too. I think horses, some of them, have a sense of humor, and I will try to prove my theory later. At any rate, we were no longer just "riders"; we were now official horse owners. So we began to make plans to build a barn in our backyard so we could have more of this one-on-one interaction.

Chapter 8

Penny

I know animal behaviorists and most people in general would scoff at my notion that horses can have a sense of humor. I believe horses are smarter than people give them credit for because they are prey animals and tend to react rather than act. I've noticed that dumb people don't have much of a funny bone, and dumb horses or horses without interaction with people don't, either. But, oh, the smart ones...

I'll give you the following scenarios and let you make up your own mind. After assuming ownership, I would go over to the stable to let Penny out. They had a large outdoor ring where they gave instructions and behind it was a huge field. Usually, when I let Penny out, she would run and buck for a few minutes and then settle down and graze. There were no other horses with her. The second time I did it, I stood watching her. She had strayed so far away I could barely see her, and I was starting to get nervous. Then the instructor came out with a class full of children. Parents sat around the perimeter watching.

All of a sudden, from the corner of my eye, I could see movement. I turned my attention to Penny and saw she was running at full gallop directly at the ring. When she got there, she came to a screeching halt and stuck her head through the bushes. That effectively scared all the horses in the ring, causing them to startle and jump around. Little children went flying off like popcorn on the stove. Parents rushed to their children. Let me be clear, no one was the least bit hurt. Everyone was a little shaken up. Penny turned tail and went back to calmly grazing.

I asked the instructor what would make a horse do such a thing.

She answered, "I'm not sure, but she probably just wanted to be with the other horses."

Well, maybe, but the other horses were still in the ring, and Penny wasn't showing the slightest interest in them now. To be on the safe side,

I walked over to her, put a lead rope on her, and returned her to her stall. She sauntered in, looking a little smug to me.

I told Rich what had happened, and he said it was strange, but we didn't know horses that well and there probably were a lot or reasons for her to do what she did. Okay.

The next day we both went to let her out. She had settled down to graze, and another class entered the ring. Her head swung around and off she went. Rich and I saw her fixating on the ring and picking up speed. We both yelled, "Whoa!" as loud as we could.

She heard us and broke stride; she knew she was supposed to stop. After that initial hesitation, however, her attention went back to the ring, and if anything, she increased speed. Before we could do anything, she screeched to a halt, stuck her head through the bushes, and once again, we had flying children. This was the second time in two days. The scenario repeated itself almost exactly. The children were fine, but the parents were upset.

I said to the instructor, "I'll just take that horse inside for you."

She wasn't about to let me get away with that, and she said, "Yes, Sandy, please remove *your* horse."

Walk of shame time again. At least it was for me. Although they don't have that vocalization, I swear, in her own way, that horse was laughing her ass off. After that, she wasn't allowed out if a class was scheduled. So she had to devise other ways to amuse herself.

She had been so wild when she first arrived that she had just about everyone intimidated and she knew it. One day, while I was watching her graze, her head came up, and she looked at me thoughtfully for a moment. She then started toward me, her speed increasing rather than decreasing the closer she got. I was on the other side of a metal gate, so I held my ground. When she got to me, she reared up and snorted, came back down, whirled around, and bucked, throwing her heels in my direction. I knew with the gate there I was perfectly safe, so I never moved. I just stood calmly. At least I was calm on the outside; inside I was a mess. She turned and looked me in the eye.

"Is that all you've got?" I said, being so much braver than I would have been if that gate hadn't been there.

She snorted one more time. I didn't move. She turned and went back to grazing, looking a little deflated. I hadn't been much fun at all. She never did that to me or anyone else again. That was fortunate because you don't always have a metal gate when you need one. Once I called her bluff and lived to tell about it, I felt reassured. She wasn't mean; she really didn't want to hurt anyone. She was just amusing herself, getting away with whatever she could. Very much like a child—a very large, potentially dangerous, thousand-pound child.

I told you that story to tell you this one. After that confrontation, I continued to release Penny into the field as long as there were no classes scheduled. One day, she wandered so far away I couldn't see her. I called, and she didn't come, but then, most of our dogs hadn't, either. I was being optimistic.

I took a lead rope and strolled toward the far side of the pasture. It had been raining heavily the prior few days. There was a muddy spot left that led into a small pond. I wasn't too concerned about it; I've ridden horses that have had a nervous breakdown when forced through a puddle. It was a beautiful day, but the owners must have been concerned about the pond. They had put up a makeshift barrier of wooden poles with burlap in between. Because of the rain, the water level was halfway up these poles.

I was still calling Penny, twirling the lead rope in the warm sun. When I spotted the pond, I also spotted our horse. I couldn't believe it; she was up to her belly in water. She was walking back and forth trying to decide if she should push through the barrier or try to go around it. I was dumbstruck, and I called out her name as loudly as I could. I was now pretty close to her. She probably hadn't heard me coming because she was so intent on the task at hand.

I effectively startled her, and she did a 180-degree turn and came blasting out of the water. The sun was blazing down onto her gleaming, wet, flame-red coat, making it look even redder. Droplets of water flew from her body, mane, and tail. Her nostrils were flared, her head and tail held high. She looked so beautiful I thought my heart would stop. I had never seen anything that breathtaking in my life.

As a matter of fact, she was so beautiful it took me a couple of seconds to realize I had been standing directly behind her and she was headed straight for me. Thank God we had already established her motives and her athleticism. She didn't have a lot of time, but when she realized I was standing there, she made a hairpin turn around me, so close water flew onto my face and arms. Once she realized it was me, she slowed, stopped, and turned around. She approached me at a walk and let out one of her welcoming nickers. When she got to me, she nuzzled my shoulder.

If it were in the cards that I was going to die anytime soon anyway, I wouldn't have minded going right then. It was one of the most perfect moments in my life. I couldn't imagine it getting any better than that.

However, just as a helpful hint, I would advise against sneaking up on really large animals and startling them. The result might not be as serendipitous as mine had been.

Once we started to give Penny the one-on-one attention she craved, her bad habits started to disappear. We certainly weren't horse trainers, but apparently, we were giving her what she needed: love, attention, and a certain amount of freedom. It didn't go unnoticed by other people, either. One of the girls that cleaned her stall, and had been a prior victim of her abuse, was waiting outside the barn when I arrived.

"Sandy, she was lying down when I went to clean her stall, and she let me pet her!"

We both beamed like idiots. This was the girl who told me I would love riding Penny. We both knew at heart that Penny was a good, sweet horse, and she was proving us right. The next day, she broke my collarbone.

Okay, she didn't really break my collarbone; it was my own fault. But I was riding her when it happened. The habit we found the hardest to cure was her tendency to bolt. Most horses will run when frightened, and when one goes, the others usually follow, sort of like mass hysteria in people. We were taking another lesson, and I was on Penny, Rich was riding another horse, and our friend Michelle was riding with us. There were probably an additional six or seven people in the ring. Michelle and I occasionally got into trouble because we would race when we weren't supposed to. This got the horses pretty excited and could be dangerous. On this day, however, we weren't doing anything wrong. Something scared one of the horses. The others where okay, but the three of us were in a group, and one of our horses became alarmed.

None of us knew which horse it was, but all three panicked and ran for the hills. Penny was the fastest, so she was out in front. Rich got his horse under control and so did Michelle. Penny and I were approaching the fence at an alarming rate, and I couldn't get her to stop. I pictured her barreling through (it was much too high to jump) and both of us being impaled on the splintered wood. I've never seen anything like that happen, but I have heard stories.

We were bearing down on the fence like a locomotive, and I was running out of options. I figured that if I couldn't stop her, I could at least turn her away from the fence. I used the entire right side of my body and tried to push her to the left. And then she just...stopped. With the momentum I had built up trying to turn her, I continued down onto the ground. I landed with all my weight on my left shoulder and, with my left ear, heard my left collarbone snap.

Everyone, including Penny, was surprised. I had just fallen off of a horse that was now standing perfectly still. And I wasn't moving. Just as a point of interest, I'd like to mention that this was October 10. My father died on October 10, and twenty-five years later, my mother died on October 10 as well. Needless to say, October 10 is not my favorite day of the year, and I always feel a little blue on that day. I had felt that way that morning and had thought about skipping riding.

Then I reasoned to myself, *Are you going stay home and feel bad, or are you going to go out and do something you love? For God's sake, take the life-affirming route.* I mean, what could happen? I was out of parents. I mulled that over as I lay in the dirt. October 10 was never going to be my favorite day. I wasn't moving because I don't like to cause a scene. I don't like being the center of attention. But I hurt like hell. Rich was the first one to get to me. He felt my arm and told me it was either dislocated or broken. I knew which, but I really didn't want to have a discussion. I sure didn't want anyone to call 911.

"Let's just go to the emergency room," I muttered.

We went to the emergency room, and they confirmed my self diagnosis. My collarbone was broken. I never had a broken bone before or since. It hurt more than I expected and took longer to heal than I would have thought. I only missed a week of work, but I was still in pain when I returned. I was just bored at home, and they were awfully shorthanded. I apologized for my absence and explained it couldn't be helped.

My boss said, "Yes it could, you didn't have to get on the damn horse."

Well, actually, I did. We were partners now. After Rich, she was my best friend. Everyone, including the instructor, said she was distraught when Rich led me to our truck and drove away. We were told that she followed the truck for as long as she could, racing along the fence that ran parallel to the driveway. They had a difficult time catching her to put her back in her stall. She hadn't meant to hurt me. It wasn't her fault. I blame myself. And October 10.

Since I've already brought up the emergency room, there was one more small incident I could mention. The outdoor arena we rode in had jumps set up for the students who were taking lessons in jumping. These were usually English riders and usually quite young. I had been interested at one point, but as I said, we got into all this rather late in life, and the coward in me had definitely bloomed. Occasionally, on trail rides, a horse I was on would hop over a branch or something, but nothing spectacular and I was able to stay with it. I had absolutely zero experience in any kind of show jumping.

I had been back from my injury for quite a while, and we were back to our lessons. On this particular Saturday, we got into a spirited game of tag on horseback. All you had to do was touch another horse or their rider and they became "it." This was grand fun for all of us, and we had been playing for a while. As she had already demonstrated, Penny was smart, and she picked up the object of the game in no time. I could tell because she was moving to cut people off before I even asked her to.

In the middle of the ring was the highest, widest jump used for the English riders. I was trying to tag someone; my plan was to race around the jump and cut them off. Penny knew the objective instinctively. She also figured she could get there quicker if she went over the jump.

I felt her gather herself under me, knew what she was going to do, and panicked. I totally forgot the word "whoa," something my friends still tease me about, and yelled at the top of my lungs, "DON'T JUMP!"

But she did. We cleared the jump beautifully, with room to spare.

The English riding students who had been standing around watching became very excited and ran into the ring yelling, "Penny can jump! Penny can jump!"

Well, that was very nice and all, but although we went over the jump together, we landed separately. I was in the dirt again. People stood around praising and patting Penny while I pulled myself to my feet. I would be sore, but I was sure nothing was broken.

I would have just popped aspirin as usual and forgotten about it, but I was scheduled for a small surgical procedure that Monday. It involved women's issues I don't want to discuss it and you don't want to read about it. However, I now had a large bruise, or hematoma, on my stomach, and I was afraid if the doctor saw it (and he couldn't miss it, as it kept getting bigger), he wouldn't proceed.

Rich suggested I go to the emergency room and get it checked out. If it was nothing, at least they would have a record of it. They could probably also tell me if it would interfere with the procedure I was having done.

Rich brought me to the hospital, and now I sat in a plastic chair in that stupid paper gown with my stupid bruise that I had brought on myself. The doctor asked what had happened.

"I fell off my horse."

"Where were you, on a trail?"

"No, we were in a training ring. I fell off going over a jump."

"Wow, you know how to jump a horse?"

"Apparently not."

I was going to add that I had no intention of jumping, that it was the horse's idea, but he seemed impressed by the middle-aged—okay, maybe elderly to him, since he looked about twelve to me—lady who was jumping horses over high obstacles. I also didn't point out that the people who knew how to jump a horse probably didn't end up in his emergency room.

After he finished his exam and took a couple of X-rays, he said I was fine. The bruise would fade, and the hospital procedure could go on as scheduled. He did have one final compliment for me though.

"I have to hand it to you, you really know how to fall."

"Thank you." I didn't add that falling, like everything else in life, is one of those things that improves with practice.

Chapter 9
Barn Building

Things were going downhill with the boarding situation. I'm not sure whose fault it was, probably mutual. Although, one mistake we made was emphasizing that we didn't know anything about horses and were counting on their expertise. This is the equivalent of taking your car in for repairs and telling the mechanic you don't know a thing about cars and just to do what is necessary. Things can get expensive pretty quickly.

They can also get ridiculous. One night, when we stopped to check on Penny, we saw she had no water. We would have happily gotten it for her ourselves, but that was not allowed at this barn. It was their water. So we told the instructor that Penny had no water. She was a kind, fun person, and I still hold a place for her in my heart. But she didn't own the facility, her parents did. She spoke to her dad and then returned to us.

Carefully not looking us in the eyes, she said, "My dad said horses don't drink water at night."

"I said we didn't know anything about horses; I didn't say we didn't know anything," I replied.

Penny got her water, but the situation became even more uncomfortable. Rich began barn building in earnest.

He already had the plans for a two-stall barn with electricity and running water. It would have a cement floor to store grain and hay, and the stalls would be dirt with rubber mats placed on top. Rich knew how to do all this work; he had done most of it on our house. So the idea of building a barn didn't intimidate him.

The reason we needed two stalls was because we weren't planning on having just Penny. We felt we needed a second horse. That way Penny wouldn't be lonely, and both Rich and I could ride together. Instead of bringing one huge, unpredictable animal into our lives, one that had already sent me to the hospital twice, we were happily planning on two. I know what you're thinking, and you're not wrong. Although Rich could build or fix just about anything, he came up short in the common sense department. Or maybe I've just rubbed off on him. The fact that we've enthusiastically agreed on every outrageous, boneheaded idea in our entire marriage is confounding.

At any rate, the barn building commenced. First, the land had to be cleared. Rich cut down the trees himself, something his father had taught him to do. The things he knows are really amazing, aren't they?

Then the stumps had to be removed, something he accomplished with the help of a borrowed excavator and a friendly neighbor.

Now came the part that involved me. The problem with people who know how to do things is they insist on doing them correctly. The correct way is almost always harder and in general a pain in the ass. Since we live in New England, Rich insisted the foundation for the barn had to be below frost level, which was about four feet down from ground level.

So it was just two middle-aged people (who were approaching elderly at warp speed) with shovels who began to dig. While we weren't exactly constructing the pyramids, we didn't have thousands of Egyptian slaves, either. Pity, really, that would have moved things along. This was not like digging at the beach. Our land was full of rocks, ledges, and huge tree roots. We started in May, just in time for the mayflies. These are tiny insects that come out in May and are so small you can barely see them; however, they bite and swarm in numbers that I would estimate somewhere in the millions. They also seem to be attracted to sweat, something we were producing by the gallons.

Rich and I were both employed, and we were spending a fair amount of time with Penny. As soon as we finished with Penny, we headed home to dig. So what was missing from our lives now? A cat, of course.

Luther lived to meet Penny. We brought him to the stable on Sundays, and they got along great. However, time was running out for him. We already had his diagnosis, and once you can see the lump, the cancer spreads like lightning to the lungs.

He had been on pain pills, but they weren't controlling it any longer. Also, with a dog that large, you are faced with the possibility of the leg collapsing and having no way to carry his huge weight to someplace that can help him.

The Decision was made, but it came heartbreakingly close to the loss of Lil' Bitty. The people I worked with couldn't help but notice the change in my demeanor. I tried not to bring it to work, but they knew what had happened, and every one of them was a kind soul. So when a stray cat showed up, they unanimously agreed that this could help ease my pain. There is also the possibility that, kind or not, they didn't want him.

This was a relatively young cat, but not a kitten by any means. He had never been neutered nor had any shots that we knew of. He was a gray-striped tiger cat that had a muscular, stocky body set atop four rather short legs. He looked like a cat version of a street fighter. Rich wanted to call him Rocky. I really didn't care. My mind was consumed by the hole in our backyard that never seemed to be getting any bigger.

Annie was working as a veterinarian technician, and when I called and told her about the cat, she said we could bring him right into her place of work. The plan was to have him fixed after hours. When we walked in, everyone gathered around the cat carrier to see the new little kitten.

As I removed him, his large body following his large head, the receptionist remarked, "That's not a kitten; that's a tom."

I didn't know what she meant, but she was going home anyway, so we didn't get into it.

The veterinarian, a woman, walked into the room and said, "Oh, you have a tom."

As she removed the cat to an operating room, with us trailing behind, I whispered to Rich, "I guess you're out of luck. He's not Rocky; he's Tommy. But I don't know how everyone but us knows that." I thought perhaps he had a name tag on him someplace that we hadn't noticed.

My daughter would explain to us later that "tom" is what they call a fully matured male cat. We didn't care. What's in a name? Unlike our dogs, we didn't even have the illusion that a cat would come when called. By that time, we had already accepted him as "Tommy," and that would remain his name.

The veterinarian was going to perform the surgery, with my daughter assisting. They usually have more help, such as an anesthetist and perhaps another technician, and the veterinarian remarked that they would need more people.

"My parents can help," chirped Annie.

"But they're not trained."

"They're fast learners." And as we were to learn later, Annie had a hot date and no intention of waiting around for more help.

Tommy was given a shot to put him to sleep, and I was given the job of holding the cone that supplied a continuous stream of anesthetic over his mouth. Rich held him in position, and the operation began. I thought I would be grossed out, but instead, I found myself fascinated by my daughter. She worked quickly, but competently and carefully.

I always thought of my children as just that—children. Her brother had married and had his own offspring, so I had to view him as an adult. Now watching my "baby" work, I had to acknowledge to myself that she was also an adult and, like my son, an admirable one at that.

"Mom, have you got that cone over his mouth?" my daughter's voice broke through my musings.

My eyes shot to my hand, and I noticed that the cone had slipped off of the side of the cat's mouth. "My God, is he waking up?" I rapidly adjusted the cone.

"No, it's just that I was getting a little woozy."

Okay, she was grown up; her brother was grown up. I obviously was a work in progress.

After the surgery, Tommy was given all the necessary inoculations, and we brought him home. Considering what had happened with Lil' Bitty, I was determined to make Tommy an "indoor" cat. Someone should have told Tommy because, up until then, I suspect he lived on the street, went where he wanted when he wanted, and was sexually probably quite the cat about town.

Perhaps because he was the only animal we now had at home, or because he was in the house all the time, I noticed more of a personality in him than other cats. And a strange personality it was. There is no polite way to say this. He was a jewel thief.

Shortly after he started living with us, I was awakened in the middle of the night by someone tugging on my finger. I opened my eyes to see Tommy with his teeth around my wedding band. Cats have teeth like needles, but his never even grazed my skin. He was methodically trying to pull my ring off my finger. As soon as he realized I was watching, he fled. Since this had happened in the middle of the night, I was left with the impression I had dreamt it. Even if I hadn't, I had no intention of bringing it up. I knew how crazy it sounded.

A few days later, as we sat watching television, I felt a tug on my sleeve. This time he was too fast for me, and he flew up the stairs with my watch in his mouth. It was a cheap watch, but we retrieved it from under the bed.

"What is he doing?" Rich asked.

I have no idea why he thought I would know, but I then related the story about the ring.

"You're kidding," he scoffed.

"Well, let's find out."

We went upstairs to where Tommy had retreated under the bed. I dragged a piece of string in front of him. No reaction. Rich swished a cat toy in front of his face. Nothing. I put my mother's pearls on the floor. He swooped down on them like an eagle on a rabbit. We took them back and continued experimenting. (He never fought us. It was like he knew it wasn't his property.)

We dragged out catnip, chew toys, and even cat treats. He couldn't care less. Put out something shiny and it was gone in a blur. We went downstairs to ponder this new development.

"What if," Rich proposed, "someone taught him to take jewelry and then put him out on the street to be adopted? And then when he has accumulated a lot of expensive things, he returns with it to that person."

We looked at each other and burst out laughing. We were mentally cataloging our valuables. If that was the plan, Tommy would indeed be with us for life. Most of our "expendable" income was now residing in the bank accounts of veterinarians. Unlike Tommy, we weren't big on jewelry. Anything with a heartbeat trumped glitter in our book.

He didn't confine his felonious activities to us, either. We had company over, and a friend who was a cat lover scooped Tommy into her lap.

"Uh, he likes jewelry," I started to warn her, all the while eyeing the expensive-looking necklace she was wearing.

"Well, that's okay, so do I," she countered.

He started to tentatively bat at the necklace.

"Look, he likes it."

No surprise there. I stood to intervene. I knew what was coming.

"He has it in his mouth. No, no, bad kitty. Give it back. He's not giving it back. Why won't he let go? Let go! Jesus, Mary, and Joseph, what's with this cat?"

By that time, I had gotten to her, literally pried Tommy's mouth open to make him release the necklace, and tucked him firmly under my arm. If it didn't belong to us, I guess he thought he had more of a claim on it.

"I don't understand. What was he trying to do?"

"Steal your necklace. I tried to warn you."

"That's the strangest thing I've ever seen."

"Not me."

"What do you mean?"

"Nothing." I had neither the time nor the energy to explain. I still had a huge hole to finish. And then a barn to build to stick on top of it.

"How did you train him to do that?"

"We didn't. We're trying to train him not to do it."

"How's it going?"

"Not well," I sighed.

As far as temperament went, Tommy was a far cry from the feral cats. Despite his rough and tumble appearance and thieving ways, he loved a good cuddle, and although his teeth and claws were formidable, we almost never saw them. He was friendly and calm and really quite a gentleman.

The only thing we butted heads on was the staying-inside rule. He wasn't used to it, wasn't buying it, and was smart enough to open the screen on the sliding glass door. We thought of putting a lock on it, but one night, we accidently locked him in the basement.

The next morning, I heard a soft meow from behind the door. I opened it, and out strolled Tommy, over a thoroughly destroyed carpet and a partially clawed solid-core door. Tearing through a screen would have been child's play. We shelved that idea and tried to just intercept him before he made an escape.

If we could get him before he slunk out, all we had to do was grab whatever part of the cat was available and haul him back in. He never retaliated, never tired to scratch or bite. He didn't even struggle. He just waited for the next opportunity. We couldn't always catch him, but when we didn't, he inevitably showed up the next morning—at 4:00 a.m. What is it with cats and 4:00 a.m.? Every one we ever had wanted out at that time or, if out, wanted in. I often wondered if there was a secret cat meeting or something. I mean, they even adjusted for daylight savings time.

With Tommy more or less integrated into the family, we were free to turn our energies to the barn-to-be. It seemed like we dug forever.

"This is going to be the hardest part, right? I mean, of the entire project, this is the worst part, right?" I was not proud of it, but I was now whining.

"Absolutely," Rich said reassuringly. He was lying through his teeth. I could almost always tell when he was lying, but I was blinded by the heat and sweat and aching muscles. However, after a particularly protracted stretch of digging, I stopped whining and gave him an ultimatum.

"I can't do this one more day in a row. I mean, we do it all week and then on the weekends, and I'm not really seeing much progress. I need a break. I don't know why you don't, but I do."

"We can't stop now. It's almost done, and we can move on to the support poles. You just can't see it because we do it every day. We have to keep going."

"I'm not doing it today. I'm warning you."

"What are you going to do?"

"Well, I'm not going to threaten to leave you. We've been married over thirty years, and you'd know it would be an empty threat." This was said with calmness and control.

Rich started to return his attention to our mutual hole.

"However," I continued while surveying the uninhabited landscape around us, "I could kill you. We have plenty of sharp tools and building equipment. It would be easy. And then I could cut up your body and strew the pieces in the woods. No one would ever find them." This was also said calmly while I surveyed our surroundings lingering on the most densely forested areas.

Now I had his undivided attention. He didn't look exactly nervous, but it might have crossed his mind that I may have become unhinged in the heat.

"Want to take in a movie?"

"Please."

And we did. I don't remember which one, but I noticed he steered away from the more violent fare that he usually preferred. And the next day, like a good little soldier, I returned to our task. He was right; that phase was just about finished. But the next one and the one after that were increasingly more difficult. As I watched him assemble the struts for the roof, I knew we would have to hoist them to the top of the barn with the excavator, a lot of muscle, and dare I say more than a dab of luck. I confronted him for the second time.

"You've been lying all along, haven't you? It was never going to get easier."

"No, it wasn't."

"Why lie?"

"You're the only help I have, and I didn't want to discourage you."

At that point, we called in the children and my daughter's boyfriend, Billy, who was a contractor. They all helped, and we even paid one of Billy's workers to finally get the damn thing done. And we did get it done, but not quite in time.

Chapter 10

Eviction

Things were deteriorating rapidly at the stable. Penny was almost always lame, and our access to her was becoming more and more limited.

The farrier put pads on her front feet and then covered them with circular horseshoes. This seemed to make her worse. I asked the instructor if having Penny let out every day might help. She agreed and said she really didn't know what else to try.

She also said they would charge extra to put Penny out for a few hours a day. I agreed to the additional fee. Now we were faced with paying her board, paying for "lessons," and paying to have her let out. We knew we would have to cut back some place, so before making the arrangements, I said that we would be dropping the lessons. If Penny was lame when it was time for a lesson, we couldn't ride her anyway, and that was what we wanted to do.

The instructor returned from a discussion with her parents and said she was sorry, but they wouldn't put Penny out for any price. They were afraid she would hurt herself and we would hold them responsible. For what? She was already lame. I suspected they didn't appreciate us giving up the lessons.

Rich and I weren't happy at this turn of events, but the barn was about half done, and we figured Penny and us would just have to tough it out until we could bring her home.

We paid her board by the month, and the day after this conversation, I came home to a message on my answering machine that said, "We have decided not to board horses any longer. Come and get your horse—immediately."

Penny was the only boarder they had at that time. They told us that they didn't usually board because the owners were pains in the ass, but that they would make an exception for us. I guess we had now slipped into that "pain in the ass" group.

We didn't have any place to put her yet, and we didn't have a horse trailer to move her. I always paid a month ahead, so I called and let them know Penny would be staying until the end of the month. They couldn't disagree; they had already cashed the check.

Now we had to find someplace to put her and some way to move her. And fast. There was a stable close to us that bred and showed Arabian horses. It was a state-of-the-art facility, and their horses were out every day. We had inquired about moving Penny there earlier, but they didn't have any room. We went back, hat in hand, and explained our situation. We told them Penny was now lame and getting worse, we had been kicked out of our present situation (I'm surprised that didn't turn into a deal breaker), and we had no place for her. We did say we were building a barn, and as soon as it was done, we would take her home.

The trainer/instructor was a lovely young girl with a heart of gold. Her parents also owned the stable she managed. They all turned out to be extraordinarily kind people. They still didn't have any room, but by rotating horses in and out, some in stalls, some in outdoor shelters, they were able to make room. They had a horse trailer (a couple, actually), and they even picked Penny up from her current residence and moved her to their place.

We again paid by the month, and they told us not to worry, as they would find a way to keep her housed until we finished our barn and could take her. When we brought her limping to them, they looked a little shocked. They had a farrier who they used and asked if we would like to have him take a look at her.

We jumped at the chance. I was unable to be there because I had to work. Rich made it a point of taking a couple of hours off so he could see what was going on. You couldn't see the inside of the hoof because of the pads. When the farrier removed them, both Rich and the owner of the stable watched. They both told me afterward that the inside of the hoof walls on both front legs were bright red. Penny must have been in agony.

The new farrier said he thought he could help her, and he did. The sores healed, and the lameness faded. The horse that loved to run, that couldn't be held back, now didn't want to move. We were told, and I believe, that she had been in pain for so long that the memory of the pain made her afraid to move around. It was suggested that we use a lunge whip (a very long stick with a rope on the end) to encourage her. Once she realized she could move without pain, then she should revert to her old self.

We used the whip and so did the people at the stable. Everyone from the owner to the instructor would take some time out of his or her day to put Penny in a huge outdoor ring and encourage her to start moving around again. By the way, they didn't charge us for this, or anything else, other than the straight room and board.

You don't hit a horse with this whip; you just point it at them, sometimes crack it behind them to get them to move. Everyone, including Rich, could make this work. Everyone but me. When I cracked the whip behind her, she walked straight past it. She would come to me, sometimes pushing the whip out of the way, and nuzzle me, much like she had that day in the pasture. Then she would rest her head on my shoulder. Sometimes she would sigh. Everyone was working hard to help her, and she was working to help herself.

When it came to me, she just sought comfort. And you know what? As long as other people could get her to do what she had to do, to become strong again, that was fine with me. Everyone and everything deserves a safe haven that they can go to without any expectations of behavior. You shouldn't have to fear being judged, just blanket acceptance. Rich and I had each other. I couldn't begrudge Penny the same kind of sanctuary. I know not everyone or everything has this luxury, but I couldn't help that. I could provide it for Penny. And I did.

Chapter 11
Incredible Razmataz

With Penny on the mend and the barn finished, we started our quest for a second horse. This is not as much fun as it sounds. Although we had owned Penny for about a year at this point, the total tonnage of what we still didn't know about horses would sink the *Titanic*. No iceberg required.

We started our search through online advertisements. We looked at a few horses, and thankfully, even our untrained eyes could spot the really crazy ones. Sometimes the horses were mean. Sometimes the owners were. And the sad part was they never seemed to match up. Some very nice people had either mean or crazy horses, and it was hard to tell them we wouldn't be helping them out. Some very nice horses had mean or crazy owners, and it was even harder leaving them in a bad situation.

I'd like to think that, like fools and drunkards, God takes special care of animal lovers. I don't know the Bible well, but I do know the passage that states (and I'm paraphrasing) that we will be judged by how we treat the least among us. Hopefully, we fall under that category, in a positive way. No way would church attendance be helping us out.

At any rate, something brought us to a horse in Massachusetts, the one that would become the next member of our family. The owners were nice people who had bought her and built a barn on their property the same way we had; however, they ran into a zoning violation, something that they believed was taken care of but turned out not to be once the horse showed up.

They had had their horse for only a couple of months. They had her vet-checked, which was something we hadn't done with Penny (she wouldn't have passed anyway), so we knew this new horse was sound. They were more than happy to give us a copy of the examination. All her shots were up-to-date, and when Rich rode her, she behaved well. They had a nine-year-old daughter, and I think the horse was for all three of them.

Her name was Incredible Razmataz, a silly name, but that was her registered name. Most horses that are registered have long, odd-sounding names. Perhaps all the cool ones were used up a century or so ago. Her owners simply called her "Raz," and that's what we called her. That, or "Razzy." She was a chestnut Appendix Quarter horse, which means she is a half-thoroughbred and half-Quarter horse.

Her markings were almost exactly like Penny's. She wasn't quite as red, and she was a little older and little larger than Penny, but you almost had to see them side by side to tell the difference. She even had the white stripe down her nose. Quite a coincidence, but they made a handsome pair.

We planned to have her picked up in a couple of weeks so we could have Penny transported home first. Penny was doing much better, but the farrier said he didn't think she would ever be a 100 percent again. That was fine with us. Penny at 80 percent would leave most other horses in the dust. She was no longer in pain; that was the main thing. We made arrangement with the new boarding facility to trailer her home.

Our barn had a Dutch door on each stall. That way we could leave the top half open and the horses could stick their heads out. When we left the entire door open, they could go into a large fenced-in paddock whenever they chose. The only time we planned on closing the barn entirely was during really bad weather. There were sliding doors on the inside of each stall that we planned to use to take the horses in and out. Those doors were heavy; I helped Rich unload them and put them in. Each door weighed over a hundred pounds but, once installed, slid relatively easily on the door track. Running the width of the middle of the barn was a narrow aisle. The inside stall doors were on one side; the other side had hay and grain stacked to the ceiling.

The paddock was enclosed by a white wooden fence, with electrical tape around the top railing—a blatant rip-off of other barns we had seen. When Penny came home, the trainer, Becca, unloaded her. Penny was pretty worked up, so Becca offered to walk her to the barn and put her in the paddock. The whole thing was beginning to overwhelm me, watching Penny dance around, wild-eyed, while taking in her new surroundings. I appreciated any help that was offered. Penny was placed securely in her new home.

Becca admired our barn and the surroundings we had made for our horses. (We still had one more coming, remember?) She said the only thing she would add would be a strip of electrical tape at the bottom of the lower rail, in addition to the one at the top rail.

I looked at the bottom rail and the distance it was from the ground and said, "But that's not that high above the ground. Surely a horse couldn't squeeze under there, could it?"

"No, but it could squeeze part of the way under and get stuck."

Okay. Point taken. The electrical tape was added around the bottom rail of the paddock the very next day.

Since I was, again, working part time, a lot the responsibility for the horses would fall on me. The day after Penny arrived, I got home from work, changed clothes, and went right for the barn to clean. Although the stall doors slid, I still found them heavy. So when I went in to clean, I opened the door just enough for me to squeeze in but not enough for a horse to fit through. People who know horses are probably already laughing.

Penny was in the paddock, and when I went out with my wheelbarrow to clean, she walked past me into the stall. I gave her a passing pat and didn't think anymore about it—until I heard the stall door being flung the rest of the way open. That was followed by the sound of hooves on concrete.

I looked up to see our horse leaving. Our house is set back quite a ways from the road and is surrounded by an old stone wall. The only opening in the wall was for our driveway. Penny headed right for it. I ran after her like a woman possessed, which hasn't actually been ruled out. I was terrified she would get to the road and be hit by a car. For those of you who have ever hit a deer or seen one hit, you know that not only is the deer a casualty, but the car is usually pretty trashed as well. An adult white-tailed deer weighs between 110 and 300 pounds. Penny weighed approximately 1,000 pounds. An accident had the potential of fatalities, and not just for Penny.

Penny wasn't racing away; she was just walking purposely toward the opening. I cut across the front of the house in order to intercept her. When she saw me coming, she upped her speed slightly. Even though she wasn't running, I couldn't catch her. She was, after all, a horse, and I was, and am, an older lady, not in the best of shape. I managed to grab onto her tail. She kept walking, but turned to look at what was dragging behind her. When she saw it was me, she didn't even speed up; she just resumed her progress.

The hair in a horse's tail is incredibly coarse, something I had never noticed until it started to slice into my hands. I had to let go. By then, Penny was at the opening of the wall, and her newfound freedom perked her up. No cars were coming, thank God.

Directly across the street from us was our closest neighbor. They were, or seemed to be, a very nice couple who had lived in the area longer than we had. They had built a beautiful log cabin. The grounds were immaculately maintained, and the gardens were lovely. Their entire property was enclosed by a rail fence. Even the driveway had a rail gate that was usually left closed. For some reason, this day it was open.

Penny made right for it and entered their property. I was relieved that she was off the road. But the relief was short lived. Once she stepped onto their lush lawn, her head went up, and she started to happily trot around and inspect the place. This caused large, ugly divots wherever her hooves dug into the soft ground. I called her name. I can't believe I was still that much of an optimist. I know she heard me, but she didn't care; she was exploring. We covered most of their property, Penny in the lead, with me breathlessly bringing up the rear. I was finally able to snag onto her halter while she stood in the middle of one of their gardens. She had petunias hanging out of her mouth and a blissful expression on her face. I was waiting for someone to come charging out of the house, possibly with a gun.

No one did, so I led Penny back to her stall. She went willingly enough. I don't think she ever intended to run away, just run around. After making sure she was secured, I walked back across the street. I rang the doorbell with the intention of apologizing and offering to fix or pay to have fixed any damage Penny had done. No one was home. I saw it as a reprieve, if only a temporary one. I would never have tried to get away with not taking responsibility. Even if I had been so inclined, it would have been impossible. The hoof prints in the lawn were more damning than any set of fingerprints could be. Plus, we were the only ones in the area with a horse.

When Rich got home that night, I explained what had happened. He had gotten home late, so he said he'd take care of it the next day as soon as he got home from work. That was really nice of him. We were both kind of weary of apologizing at this point.

Rich arrived home earlier than I did the next day. When I pulled into the driveway, I saw him, our neighbors, and Penny. They were gathered around her with carrots and apples.

When I started to apologize, they gushed, "You brought your horse home!"

At this point, they were happier about it than I was. They shrugged off any attempts on our parts to apologize, also flatly refusing any efforts to fix or pay for damages done. They said she really hadn't done any harm at all. Lord, had they not seen their lawn? Both they and Rich were beaming happily. In my mind, they went from what I thought of as a "nice couple" to grade-A, top-of-the-line, perfect neighbors. And damn good sports. They remain that way to this day.

Now that Penny was settled in, it was time to bring Raz home. We still didn't have a trailer. We didn't think we would need one. Once we had the horses home, we figured we could just ride them to nearby trails. Ignorance really is bliss. Becca and her husband, Matt, got the honor of transporting Raz. We paid them but, to my mind, not nearly enough. Becca also thought it was time to give me a lesson on "herd dynamics," one more thing I knew absolutely nothing about. Up until then, I hadn't even heard the term.

Apparently, when more than one horse shares the same space, one is dominant and the others submissive. This means the dominant one would be the boss and the other ones, or one in our case, would back off and let the dominant one have its way. Becca knew how much I loved Penny, but she warned me that this was not a decision we would be making. The horses would decide, and we would have to live with it. In a herd, the older and larger animal is usually the dominant one. That meant Raz. I didn't think Penny would tolerate being pushed around by anything or anyone; however, instinct is a pretty strong motivator.

I asked how the dominant horse was established and how we would know which one it was. Becca smiled and assured us we would know. She said there would be a confrontation, probably over food. They would get fed their grain twice a day in their individual stalls. That probably wouldn't be an issue. But once in the paddock, no matter how many piles of hay I put out, the dominant horse would probably chase away her counterpart—at least until the submissive horse understood that she wasn't the one calling the shots. This might be accomplished with snarky looks and bared teeth. Or it could escalate to kicking, biting, or even an all-out donnybrook.

Once the pecking order was established, it usually endured for the length of the relationship between the horses, unless additional horses were added to the mix. That was at least one thing we didn't have to worry about. Two horses would be our limit. I'm not sure of much, but that you could take to the bank. I already felt we had taken on more than we could handle. Plus, the whole battling for dominance deal—I could never have conjured that up in my wildest nightmare. A lot of my ideas about the larger animals had come from Walt Disney.

Before bringing home Raz, we had her back shoes removed. We did the same thing with Penny. That way, as Becca said, they couldn't kick a hole in each other. *A HOLE?* I know she didn't mean it literally, but still, good God in heaven, what had we gotten into?

Raz was brought home and let into the paddock where Penny was munching hay. They seemed delighted to see each other and soon were racing around the enclosure, bucking and jumping as happy as two clams—if, you know, clams could run and jump. As I stared at 2,000-plus pounds of muscle rocket around our backyard, I felt my stomach sink.

Becca leaned over, put her hand on my arm, and said quietly, "You know we are just around the corner. You're not alone."

I believe I thanked her then, but if not, I want to publicly thank her now. She could never imagine how much those words meant to me.

This happened on a weekday, and after the initial introduction, we decided to keep the horses separated at least until the weekend when we would both be home. As Rich said, in case they started fighting, there would be two of us to break up the hostilities.

I didn't want to handle it alone, so I appreciated the thought, but even with two of us, what were we supposed to do if it got really ugly? I mean, these were not hamsters. We couldn't just pluck them up by the scruff of their necks. Personally, the only way I would have been comfortable was if we had the back-up power of the Texas Rangers. Actually, hamsters were starting to sound like a good idea.

Saturday arrived, just like days do when you really don't want them to. I placed six piles of hay in the paddock, and Rich took the horses in one by one. Penny started to munch on one pile of hay, Raz on another. Only a few minutes went by when Raz sauntered over to where Penny was eating. Raz bared her teeth and flattened her ears back against her head. Penny moved on to a different pile. After a few minutes, Raz moved to that pile, and Penny moved on again. This went on for an interminable amount of time, but no one had been bitten or kicked, so I wasn't complaining.

Rich and I sat on the back stairs and watched them, ready to spring into action if needed. What exactly we would do hadn't been discussed. I suspect because neither of us had any idea. We not only didn't have a back-up plan, we didn't have a plan.

We stared at them until our eyes went blurry, but nothing dramatic happened. Then, just when the sun set and we could barely see, Penny revolted. She kicked Raz in the chest and ran like hell. Raz took off after her, and although we couldn't see anything with the fading light and all the dust that was kicked up, we heard the thud of hooves when they connected with the other horse. We didn't know who was getting kicked, and the horses were not crying out or making any sounds, except for the occasional grunt when struck. It was just running and kicking from what we could tell.

I took the lack of screaming as a positive sign. A screaming horse can turn your blood to ice and your bowels to water. Once the dust settled, they both went back to eating at different hay piles. There didn't appear to be any blood. No one seemed seriously hurt. If Raz occasionally moved to Penny's pile, Penny moved off. They both seemed to have accepted the situation. Raz would be the dominant horse, and that was that. Or so everyone thought. At any rate, I had to go lie down.

Because we had her papers, unlike Penny, we knew all of Raz's history. Until she came to us, she had never stayed at the same place for more than two years. At one point, she had been used as a lesson horse.

There is nothing wrong with lesson horses, except sometimes, after being ridden by a lot of different people with a whole range of abilities, they pick up tricks of their own. Raz sure had. When you tried to get on her, she waited until you had your foot in the stirrup and then swung her body away. You either sped up or fell on the ground. This habit was actually pretty easy to break once she realized we weren't going to tolerate it. But she didn't stop testing us or our abilities for quite some time.

The first day I was home alone with her turned into a fairly memorable one. Penny respected your personal space. Raz did not. She shoved and bullied her way around, sort of like some of those women you see during a final sale in Filene's bargain basement. I had cleaned her stall and was in the process of closing the door. There was a small gap left, but I wasn't about to make the same mistake I made with Penny. As Raz approached the door, I hurried to shut it. She got there in time to stick her nose through. I stepped forward to protect the door, so she shoved my head instead. I don't think it was on purpose, but my head hit the metal frame of the door. Although I was seeing stars, I was able to push her nose back in and shut and lock the door.

A little woozy, I finished my chores and headed back to the house. I glanced in the mirror and saw my left eye start to discolor. Wonderful. My first day with Penny and she escaped. My first day with Raz and she gives me a black eye, the first one I had ever gotten in my life. Plus, I had a pounding headache. I felt the need to lie down again.

I had fallen asleep, but heard Rich when he came home from work. My hair was fairly long then, so I pulled it over my discolored eye and turned my face toward the back of the couch.

Mr. Enthusiasm bounced in and said, "Want to go riding?"

"Not now, I'm tired and have a headache."

"Well, I'm going to try the new horse." This was said a little resentfully. I think he expected more eagerness on my part.

"Knock yourself out." I didn't add that I didn't have to knock myself out. Raz had done it for me.

I fell back to sleep. Or I may have gone unconscious. I can't be sure; I never had it checked out.

When I woke up, I didn't see or hear Rich nor did I see either of the horses. That was odd. I opened the front door and saw dozens of hoofprints gouged into the lawn. *I had gotten Raz secured, hadn't I?* I thought I had, but I couldn't have sworn to anything.

I called to Rich, and he came out of the barn. Both horses straggled into the paddock after him. Besides the paddock, we had put up a large "round pen" on the other side of our property. This was to be used to work out the horses. It was made of sections of metal bars that we assembled into a circle.

As soon as Rich saw me, he started to shout, "I took Raz down to the round pen to lunge her before riding, and you won't believe what she did. She lunged fine, but when I opened the gate to take her out, she blasted past me. Knocked me right over. I'm surprised she didn't trample me, the big bitch! I mean it, Sandy, you wouldn't have believed it!"

I pulled back my hair so he could get a look at my eye.

"Oh."

"Yeah, how did you get her back?"

"When she got to the front lawn, she stopped to graze. Do you think she's mean?"

"No," I sighed, "I think she's just a pushy horse and we'll have to put some time in with her to teach her some manners. Remember how Penny used to be?"

"Penny was never pushy."

"No, she was just flat-out crazy. But she isn't anymore. She's sweet as can be and has really bonded with us. But it didn't happen overnight."

"Could be you're right."

Could be. It was bound to happen eventually.

Since we now had both horses installed in their new surroundings, we decided to go on a trail ride that weekend. Our street is actually an interstate and is paved; however, the Rhode Island–Massachusetts border is just a quarter of a mile north. Soon after crossing the border, there are entrances into Douglas State Forest that bring you to dirt trails winding through the woods. We only had to walk the horses a very short distance to get them off the highway. Sounds easy, doesn't it?

Our street doesn't have a lot of traffic usually, but some of the cars and trucks that use it are moving way above the speed limit. We decided to go early on Sunday morning. That way we hoped to not see any traffic at all. Rich was riding Raz, and I was riding Penny. It was a lovely morning, and as we moved out, we didn't see any cars. Things were looking good.

However, when we got to the Massachusetts line, both horses refused to go any farther. I'd like to say they just stopped, but that would be out of character for these two. They both began dancing around, moving sideways, tossing their heads, and acting distinctly nervous.

We surveyed our surroundings to try to see what could be spooking them. On one side were a house and a man in the front yard raking leaves. On the other side were just trees. Rich and I looked at each other and shrugged. We didn't see anything that should scare a horse, not ever a hypersensitive horse. We turned them in circles and tried to reassure them that everything was fine and we had the situation well in hand. We stroked their necks and talked encouragingly to them. They weren't buying it, and we were getting frustrated. We could practically see the turnoff for a trail. And a car was bound to come along eventually.

We steeled our reserves and kicked them forward. Well, we wanted them to go forward. They went backward—at a pretty impressive speed, too. We tried again and only succeeded in getting them to the same spot, but not an inch farther.

Suddenly, Rich said to me, "Sandy, look up!"

The power line from the pole to the house where the man was raking leaves must have shorted out. At any rate, there were sparks, and a small fire was just starting in an overhanging tree. Rich rode over to the man and pointed up. He thanked us and rushed into the house. Okay, so the horses had a point. And it was lucky for the homeowner that they were going by. Now that we knew what it was, we could continue our ride. At least we thought so.

I mean, it wasn't a raging inferno; we could easily go around it. Or so we thought. Not on these horses. They weren't having it. We finally turned them around and went in the opposite direction. This was heading toward what we laughingly call the "center of town," and there wouldn't be any trails to ride. We no longer had a destination in mind, but the horses were moving, going frontward and everything, so we decided to just keep going for a bit.

A neighbor saw us and came out to look at the horses. While we were chatting amicably, a car drove slowly up the street. When the driver saw us, she pulled over and stopped. I heard something in the distance. The horses were dancing again.

The driver said, "It's not my business, but I just came from the center of town, and there are fire trucks right behind me. I'd get those horses off the road."

Of course she would, because she was smart, probably smart enough to realize that if you tell someone they have a fire, they will be calling the fire department, and hopefully trucks will come. She wouldn't have been on that road at all. Now the sirens were clearly audible, and the horses were close to hysterical. The back of our property was all woods, and by cutting through the neighbor's yard, we were able to dash out of the way, through the woods, and back to the barn. We hadn't gone very far at all.

It was a disappointment, but we weren't about to give up. The fire was small, and we knew the trucks wouldn't be there long. We went in and had lunch, waited a while after we saw the trucks leave, and decided to try it again.

We rode to the opening in the stone wall to go out into the street. The horses stopped. This time there was no nervous jumping or dancing; they just stood still. It didn't matter what we did; they wouldn't move out onto the road. We may not have given up, but they had. They didn't trust us. We were supposed to be in charge. We were their leaders. We had obviously blown it. They knew we were idiots, and this wasn't instinct; they had proof. We had told them everything was fine, nothing to be afraid of. Well, in their minds, they were probably thinking, "Yeah, nothing to be afraid of—except for the freaking FIRE!"

We didn't get them on the road that day, but we are nothing if not persistent. The following day, they trusted us a bit more—not necessarily because of anything we did, more likely because, like all our other animals, we were all they had. And like it or not, eventually you have to leave the yard.

As the summer progressed and we had the occasional run-in with an idiot driver or a pack of motorcycles, we decided to spring for a horse trailer. That way we didn't have to take them on the road at all. Don't get me wrong, most drivers were courteous and would stop and wait until we passed. Motorcycle riders were even more inclined to be polite, perhaps feeling more vulnerable than their counterparts in cars. However, there was always the occasional person who thought it was an absolute riot to blow his or her horn, gun the engine, or blast past us. Some were just ignorant of what could happen. Some seemed to enjoy seeing the horses rear up or try to bolt. We didn't enjoy either.

While this was going on, our daughter, unbeknownst to us, was facing her own animal conundrum. When she and her boyfriend moved in together, he already had a cat. Annie was still working as a veterinarian technician, and she was always bringing home strays, fostering them and then finding them homes. One little guy had been tossed in a dumpster. He was only a kitten, and she named him Cooter. I don't know what the name means, either, but it was her cat, who am I to question?

Anyway, finding Cooter a permanent home would be a challenge because of his aggressive disposition. So, of course, she adopted him. As soon as she brought him home, however, Billy's cat had a kitty nervous breakdown. They thought it would get better with time. It didn't. Billy's cat was shy and reserved, and the new addition was a bit of a hellion. He didn't play well with others, either. As he grew, the situation only deteriorated. It got to the point where Billy's cat was getting physically ill.

When they wanted to go on vacation, we agreed to babysit Cooter. I didn't have any idea if he would get along with Tommy, but the one thing

I was sure of was Tommy could hold his own. Cooter was still young, but pretty much full grown by this point. When we brought him home, he spied Tommy and took off after him. Tommy never turned to run. He just stood there with his "bring it on" attitude, the tip of his tail twitching ominously. This threw the newcomer for a loop. He stopped short when he got to Tommy.

Once they got used to each other, there was a lot of "play" fighting, although it sounded and looked authentic enough, swiping at each other until they were rolling around on the floor in what looked like a fight to the death. Then, after a few minutes, they would knock it off and go explore something, usually with Tommy in the lead.

Unlike Billy's cat, Tommy was not the least bit intimidated, and if he didn't always enjoy a sneak attack, it didn't come close to unnerving him. On the other hand, my nerves were becoming more frayed every day. They both had all their claws and all their teeth, and why there was never any blood or injuries was a bit of a mystery.

I always expected to come home from work to some sort of bloody carnage, but it never happened. Tommy even began sneaking Cooter outside with him. Cooter would follow him into the woods; they would do whatever cats do in the woods and walk back out, Cooter trailing closely behind Tommy.

One day, Tommy came back alone. I called out for Cooter and heard an answering meow, but couldn't tell which direction it was coming from. And, apparently, he couldn't figure out where I was, either. After watching this futile effort for a bit, Tommy disappeared into the woods again and came out a few minutes later with Cooter following behind him. It was settled; Cooter was now Tommy's responsibility. We never said we would adopt him, but we told Annie and Billy he could live with us.

The house and our lives were getting full again, with horses, cats, the hummingbirds, and various wildlife. Rich had a birthday coming up, and I asked what he would like.

"You know, it's really not the same without a dog."

"You want another dog? Really? What would be your second choice?"

"I don't have one." (He obviously was not going to make this easy for me.) "Anyway, why not a dog? You love dogs."

"Two horses and two cats aren't enough for you?" I couldn't help thinking, *Especially when they all seemed on the brink of hostilities.*

"I didn't say that. I just said it seems like something is missing without a dog. Don't you feel it?"

Uh, actually, I didn't. As much as I love dogs, I was tired of caring for and cleaning up after animals. I was working all day, getting older by the minute, and two cats didn't seem like twice the work; they seemed like quadruple the work. Two horses seemed like an entire herd. Plus, I didn't have the heart to outlive another canine companion. Although I was getting older, I wasn't old enough to reasonably expect to make my exit before a dog. Our bullmastiffs never made it past seven or eight. The average life expectancy is under ten years for that breed. They just don't live very long. Our German shepherds did better, but still aged fairly quickly.

Both our daughter and our veterinarian were huge believers in "mixed-breed vigor." Annie suggested we go to the town animal shelter and pick a dog that was not huge, but not tiny, either, a dog that was the result of at least a couple of different breeds. She was convinced a dog like that would live longer. Our veterinarian concurred. Also, I liked the idea of rescuing a dog. I just didn't like the idea of another dog, or any other animal, at that point. I agreed in principle and hoped that Rich would forget about the entire thing.

Rich's birthday came and went without any new additions. I was just starting to relax when he plopped our local newspaper down in front of me.

"There's our new dog!"

I looked at the black-and-white picture of a shelter dog of indeterminate breed. All I could tell from the picture was he had a pointy nose, floppy ears, smallish eyes, and what appeared to be black-and-white fur. That's not what Rich saw.

"Doesn't he have a great smile?"

Well, his mouth was open in what appeared to be a goofy sort of grin; I don't know if I would have called it a "smile" exactly, but I agreed to go look at him.

Chapter 12

Dudley

We called the shelter and were told that they couldn't keep this particular dog on their premises because it had never had any shots or been neutered. We would have to go to the home of the people who were putting him up for adoption. We were given an address in the town of Woonsocket. We called ahead, and when we got there, the owners were out front waiting for us.

They lived on the third floor of a tenement; there was a tiny grass-and-dirt yard that contained two adult dogs and one half-grown puppy. All three dogs were happily playing with an empty plastic bottle. We were told that the older dogs were the parents (I couldn't have told you what breed either of these two were) and that they had had a litter of puppies. All the puppies had found homes, but this one had been brought back and needed to be readopted. That should have been a red flag.

The people who owned these dogs were really young (they seemed like kids to us), but were probably in their early twenties. That they loved their dogs was obvious. None of them seemed abused or neglected. If anything, they seemed happy and healthy. How they pulled that off in a third-floor apartment was amazing in itself. However, since the puppy had never even seen a veterinarian, we suspected they were in a bit over their heads.

As I watched the puppy play, I was able to get a better look at him. His face was black with a strip of white that covered his head, except for a black spot right on the top. We joked that this must be his on/off button. If only. The white continued down between his eyes and covered his entire nose. He also had a white ruff around his neck that ran down between his front legs and onto his belly. The rest of him wasn't exactly black; it was black with brown striping, or what is called "brindle" in the dog world. He had four white paws. The very tip of his long tail was white, and he carried it high and at a jaunty angle. All and all, he was a handsome little dude.

Those were the positives. The negatives, which I couldn't ignore, were the breeds I suspected comprised him. He most resembled a border collie. Border collies are probably the smartest breed, but they are working dogs. They have a tremendous amount of energy and stamina. While they can make good pets, they are not terribly outgoing with people. They are much happier herding sheep or cattle. They require a lot of exercise, for both mind and body.

I wasn't crazy about any of that in our particular circumstances. The part that really made my heart sink was the only other breed that I thought I recognized in this puppy. He had to be part American Staffordshire terrier, or as more commonly known, pit bull. You couldn't help but see it in the set of his ears (rather far back on his head) and the small, if intelligent-looking eyes. The brindle coloring is also common in pit bulls.

Rich doesn't believe any dog, no matter what the breed, is born mean. I don't, either. He also believes that any dog can be made mean, and I agree with that as well. The problem with pit bulls is that they have been systematically bred to be aggressive. When they bite, unlike other dogs, they will not let go.

In one Rhode Island town, if you are found to be "harboring" a pit bull, you are subject to a $250 fine and not more than thirty days in prison. Do I think this law is ridiculous, unfair, and overreaching? Of course I do. Does it nag at the back of my mind? You bet it does. However, the puppy we were looking at might not have any pit bull in him at all. I could be wrong. I certainly had a history of it. Nevertheless, neither of the breeds that I thought I recognized in this little guy would be a good fit.

If it were just Rich and me, it would make more sense. The puppy was hyper and would probably exhaust us, but even if he had been 100 percent pit bull, I wouldn't have been frightened of him. The problem was our grandchildren. My son and his wife, Pam, have three beautiful daughters. Two were about six years old at the time, and the baby was under a year. Most dog-bite victims are children. All three girls were terrified of dogs. Most holidays were spent at our house. The more I thought about it, the less attractive the whole idea seemed.

However, the owners seemed to think that because we had shown up, we had already made up our minds. Rich harbored the same assumption. When I opened the truck door to get a sweater, the puppy jumped in and happily ensconced himself in the rear seat. Seems like I was alone in not considering it a done deal. I pushed down my misgivings and climbed into the truck. Rich joined us, and off we went.

On the ride home, Rich was grinning from ear to ear. The puppy was wagging his tail and poking his nose through the opening in the front bucket seats. Okay, I was probably wrong about everything. Even if I wasn't, the look on Rich's face sealed the deal. I thought about this man who I had married so many years ago, who worked so hard without complaint. When he reached his midlife crisis years, did he fall for fast women or fast cars?

No, he fell for a fast red mare that he knew I loved as much as he did. I always knew he had a weakness for redheads with long legs. He had been engaged to one before I met him. I used to think if my marriage were vulnerable, that would be the weak link. It apparently was. I just thank God that the redhead he fixated on was a horse.

At any rate, as we traveled toward home, with our new puppy in tow, I could feel myself start to smile. The whole thing was probably a huge mistake. It wouldn't be our first. And for some reason, they all seemed to work out in the end.

The puppy had already been named. They called him "Tank." We had a couple of dogs (the bullmastiffs come to mind) that would have easily fit that name, not this dog, though. We kept glancing at him in the rearview mirror. He had the same loopy grin and an eager-to-please attitude.

"He doesn't look like a 'Tank,'" Rich said. "More like a Norman."

"Or maybe an Elliot or a Dudley," I chimed in.

"Dudley," Rich repeated.

We didn't usually change our animals' names if they had them, as we didn't want to confuse them. But this was just not a Tank.

The decision was made; we renamed him on the way home. In the months to come, we extended the original name to terms of endearment such as "The Dudster," "Dudley D. Dog," and the most popular, "Duddie." We called him a few other things as well, but they weren't terms of endearment, and there is no point in dwelling on them.

When we walked through our front door, the cats disappeared like smoke. I thought I saw a tail disappearing up the stairs to the bedrooms. I assumed they would be hiding under the bed. Dudley was used to stairs, so he bounded up ours, but I'm not sure if he had seen the cats run up them or not. He certainly didn't know they were lying in wait. He made it to the top stair, and both cats jumped on him from opposite directions.

I don't know if it was the force of the cats or the element of surprise, but the poor little guy tumbled down the entire flight of stairs. I ran to pick him up, while the cats strutted away. Dudley wasn't hurt, but he seemed a little confused. I don't think he knew what hit him. He started up the stairs again, but Rich scooped him into his arms.

"That's enough of a welcoming party for now, buddy; let's go outside for a bit."

We brought a rubber ball for him to play with. We gently rolled it away from him, and he started bounding after it. He had a bit of a silly, awkward run, probably a by-product of border collie legs and a very broad pit bull chest. It made us smile. Then he looked past the ball and spotted the horses. You could almost see a cartoon bubble over his head with the word "Cool!" imbedded in it. He bounded toward the paddock. His herding instinct must have kicked in full force. Nothing awkward about this run, he moved like a streak of lightning.

You can herd cattle, you can herd sheep, but unless you're a stallion, it's best to leave the mares alone. Dudley didn't know that, and we weren't nearly fast enough to stop him. He dashed under the lower rail, surprising the horses, making them run. They were at a full gallop, and he was almost fast enough to keep up. We couldn't get near enough to any of them to help. Once the horses realized what they were running from, they did a 180-degree turn and started chasing him. He was delighted, all part of a grand game to him. They didn't look like they were playing to us.

At one point, they overtook him, and he was actually running under them and between their legs. Rich and I held our collective breath. Finally, he began to tire and drop back, giving us the opportunity to snag him out of harm's way. We took him back into the house, and he happily hopped onto the leather couch in the family room and stretched out.

I know I said we didn't allow our animals on the furniture, but poor little Dudley had only been with us for a couple of hours, and during that entire time, *something* was trying to kill him. We didn't have the heart to tell him to get down.

However, as he rested happily on our good couch, we couldn't help noticing the resumption of his grin, wider now than ever, and his slowly wagging tail.

"I can't believe it," I said. "Since he's been here, four animals have tried to murder him, but I've never seen a happier, more-contented-looking dog."

"I think it's all the attention. I swear he thinks he's popular," Rich countered.

The more we got to know Dudley, the more likely it seemed that Rich had nailed it. I believe that with dogs, as with children, they prefer negative attention to no attention at all. As each day passed, we would find more and more quirks with this special little dog. Having been returned after adoption once already, we would never consider bringing him back. He already suffered terribly from separation anxiety. But that was only one of his "issues."

Or, as Billy observed, "He didn't have issues; he had the whole subscription."

We had gotten him on the weekend, and at least we were home to referee. But I had to go back to work on Monday, and including the commute, it would be a ten-hour day. We were told that he was housebroken, and he never had an "accident" in the house and hasn't to this day. My concern about leaving him in the house while at work was more the cats than accidents. Ten hours is a lot to expect from a puppy. At the time, I just thought if he couldn't wait, I would just clean it up.

However, the thought of the cats doing serious damage to him made me uneasy, just one of the reasons I had believed from the beginning that we were becoming over-stocked in the animal department. We knew we couldn't lock the cats in one room. There simply wouldn't be a room left.

The thought of coming home to a torn and shredded puppy was more than I could handle.

We still had the enclosure around the deck that we had used for Luther when he was left outside. It contained the deck and three shade trees with a doghouse underneath. I would make sure food, water, and toys were in plentiful supply. Still, ten hours seemed awfully long to leave a young, newly acquired dog outside.

We decided to do a trial run the very first day we had him. After his rest on the couch, I threw a treat into the enclosure. I wasn't concerned about the fence; it was chain link and in perfect condition.

Dudley bounced out after the treat and, once he swallowed it, started to explore.

I moved from the back of the house to the front to set the dining room table. Through the window, I caught I glimpse of movement on the front porch. I opened the front door to see what it was, and in came Dudley. *Had I not shut the gate?* I was almost sure I had. Maybe it wasn't locked. I went to check, and Dudley followed closely behind. The gate was shut and locked. Nothing looked out of place. I once again left Dudley in the enclosure and returned to the dining room. Dudley beat me to the front door.

I called to Rich and told him what was going on. We were at a loss to understand what was happening. He couldn't have dug his way out. He hadn't had the time, and there was no telltale tunnel under the fence. He couldn't have possibly jumped it; the fence was four feet high. Rich told me to put him out again and walk to the front of the house, while he watched Dudley. He stood in the window, while I proceeded to the front door. I opened the door, and in walked Dudley.

Rich strolled over. "Mystery solved."

"How is he getting out?"

"He's climbing the fence."

"What do you mean he's climbing the fence?"

"Just that. He scrambles over the fence like a little military commando."

"I think commandos have equipment, ropes and things."

"Okay, he's climbing over the fence like a little commando—without the equipment."

"They also have a lot of training."

"Apparently, he doesn't need it."

"Do you think it would help if the fence were taller?"

"Not from what I saw. He'd just climb higher and take a little longer."

Okay, the enclosure wasn't going to do it. I just didn't know what to do. I didn't want to leave him in with the cats. Leaving him outside was now out of the question. We decided to sleep on it. Maybe we would figure something out the next day. We still had Sunday before we had to go back to work.

Dudley's separation anxiety had already manifested itself. He would lie in front of the bathroom door when one of us needed to use it. He wanted to keep us in sight as much as possible. When I went to take my shower that night, I used the bathroom at the top of the stairs. Dudley had been playing with Rich, and I didn't think he saw me leave.

As I was toweling off, I heard Rich's voice outside the bathroom.

"Don't worry, Duddie, there are no windows in that room, and you're guarding the only door. She has to come out eventually."

And of course I did, but I was already becoming pretty tired. It had been a long, stress-filled day. We decided to put Luther's dog bed right up against our bed on my side. That way I could put a reassuring hand on Dudley while he drifted off to sleep. I know it was Rich's dog, but he was the one with the full-time job; mine was part time, so if the adjustment period was protracted, I could afford to lose sleep more than he could.

As Dudley drifted off to sleep, I found myself following his lead. Rich was already snoring. About an hour later, something crashed onto the bed with the force of a cannonball. It jolted us both wide awake, and Rich doesn't wake easily. As I tried to calm my racing heart, I watched Dudley contentedly settle down between us.

"We have to nip this in the bud," Rich said.

I agreed, and Rich walked around the bed and called Dudley.

"Come on, buddy, out you go. This is your bed," he said, pointing at the dog bed on the floor.

He didn't have to pull Dudley out of our bed. Dudley obligingly hopped out and went back to his bed. Okay, that wasn't too bad. We both went back to sleep.

BOOM! a second assault on our bed. Let me make this clear. He was not just hopping up on the bed nor was he climbing up (something we now knew he was an expert at). He was hurtling himself up and landing with all the power and impact of a small piano. It was also interesting that he waited until we were sound asleep to make his move. Okay, it wasn't interesting then, but it is in retrospect.

At this point, I think I should tell you that our "little dog" would eventually be sixty-five pounds of pure muscle, and at five months, he was well on his way. When friends came over to see him, they were expecting something the size of a Chihuahua or Lhasa apso. They tried to gently explain that only we would consider this a "little dog." Well, they were probably right. We were used to the larger breeds. However, if anyone had witnessed him running with the horses like we had, I think they would have seen him as little as well.

The second time, we didn't even bother to get out of bed; we just pointed to his bed, and he very obligingly returned to it.

The third time, we had been sleeping a bit longer, both falling into an exhausted slumber. This time, he hit the bed so hard he almost bounced us out. We both stared at him through bleary, bloodshot eyes. He was happily making a nest for himself at the bottom of the bed.

"Do you really care that much if he sleeps at the bottom of the bed?" Rich asked.

My heart was still pounding with adrenaline from the last abrupt awakening.

"Not that much."

"Me either. I think we should leave him there before one of us has a heart attack."

Dudley snuggled down into the covers, and we dropped limply back onto our pillows. It occurred to me that we hadn't had him for one full day yet, and I was already contemplating killing myself. Or Rich. Definitely the cats.

On Sunday, we figured we would put a baby gate up in the doorway of the spare bedroom. We moved the cats, their litter boxes, and food and water into that room. They could easily jump the gate; I was hoping they wouldn't with Dudley on the other side. Dudley could have gotten into the bedroom, but I was hoping the cats would keep him out. We didn't have a lot of options. We both had to go to work. Since my job was part time, Monday was the only day that was ten hours long. The rest of the week was usually four or five hours a day.

When I got home on Monday evening, Dudley was lying on one side of the couch, and Tommy was stretched out on the other. Okay, the rule about no animals on the furniture was now just wishful thinking. I knew the cats went wherever they wanted when we weren't home. Shedding is a dead giveaway. Now that Dudley had broken the barrier, I guess Tommy felt he could come out in the open. Cooter was behind the gate, looking distinctly sullen.

It looked like Tommy and Dudley could be friends someday. I mean, they weren't yet, but they tolerated each other. That was too much to hope for with Cooter. At least everyone was okay, so it was fine with me.

I was amazed that the only thing Dudley had gotten into the entire day was the phone book. That was completely chewed up and destroyed. But we don't call that many people anyway. I had one other trick (besides allowing them to destroy the house) to keep a lonely dog busy in my arsenal, but it didn't work with Dudley. They sell a dog toy called a "Kong" or a "Budda Ball," depending on what brand you get. This is sort of an elongated ball made out of some kind of indestructible rubber, and it has an opening at one end. The idea is to cram as many dog treats as you can, as tightly as possible, into the toy. Then, when you leave, you give the toy to the dog. It would take Luther about two hours to work all the treats out.

I prepared the ball for Dudley and gave it to him on Monday morning. Instead of settling down with it, he shook it once, cocked his head, and then ran to the top of the stairs. Once there, he flung the ball down the stairs. As it bounced off every step, treats came flying out. He had them all gobbled up before the ball stopped bouncing. He looked at me as if to say, "Now what?"

Damned if I know, Dudley, damned if I know.

A close friend of mine owned a border collie, and I called for guidance.

She didn't sound surprised and said, "Yup, that sounds like a border collie, all right. Try making the ball up the night before. Then put it in your freezer. That way he can't get the treats out all at once; he'll have to work at it until they start to thaw."

And, son of a gun, it worked. It's something we still do to this day.

His previous owners told us the only thing they had taught him was housebreaking (and he was) and to stand *between* your legs when he needed to go out. I don't know why anyone would teach a dog this. It's not as bad as humping your leg, but the dog was getting taller, and I'm short and haven't been growing for quite some time. I took to lunging for the door whenever I was wearing a skirt, or if we had company, so I could get it open before he had a chance to "tell" me he wanted to go out. Not his fault, but irritating as hell. I've never been able to entirely break him of the habit. It doesn't bother Rich, but then, he's a full foot taller than I am. As so often happens, Dudley rarely does this to Rich, but gives me the full benefit of this particular "trick."

On the positive side, I taught him to sit down, stay, and come in about a day and a half. They're not kidding when the say border collies are smart. I couldn't wait to show Rich when he came home.

"Tell him to do something."

"Dudley, lie down."

Dudley hit the ground like he had been shot. Rich agreed that was pretty impressive. However, Dudley was staring intensely at him, a quivering ball of expectation and energy.

"Why is he looking at me like that? What does he want?"

"He wants to know what you want him to do next."

"That's what I want him to do next."

"For the rest of the night?"

"Yeah, I'm tired, and that's what Luther did."

"Sorry to burst your bubble, but he's not tired. He's been resting all day, he's young, and he's not Luther."

"Well, what am I supposed to do? Lord knows we haven't gotten any sleep."

"You wanted another dog."

"I guess I could throw the Frisbee around for him."

We found out that Dudley was a world-class Frisbee chaser; the only thing he was better at was chasing deer. Sometimes he chased them clear out of state. He knew the word "come," but like most dogs, he had selective hearing when something interesting caught his attention. Unlike the horses, the deer took off every time.

We couldn't fence in our entire five acres; besides, he'd probably just climb over it. We couldn't seem to stop or even dampen his "chase" instinct, either. He always came back, exhausted and happy, but our town, like most towns, has a leash law. Also, dashing through the woods could be dangerous, especially during hunting season. We took to putting a really long rope on him when playing Frisbee, and when he spied something that made him bolt, we tried to get to the end of the rope before it was out of our reach. Our average was about fifty-fifty, not nearly good enough, and he was getting faster. Or we were getting slower.

We had set up an appointment for the veterinarian the first week. He would get all his shots and be neutered. I hoped neutering would calm him some and figured I could ask the professionals about some of his behaviors that puzzled me.

The weirdest one was his propensity to stand on his hind legs like a person. I don't mean he jumped up on the counters or chairs and leaned. He would be in the middle of a room and, all of a sudden, hop to his hind legs and stand there, with his front paws held at chest level. His sense of balance was phenomenal. I had never seen anything even close to this before, and I had no idea how or why he did it. He didn't move around, didn't hop or walk forward. He just stood there, like he was waiting for a bus.

I pulled out one of our dog books and tried to see if there was any information or precedent for this particular quirk. Lord knows I didn't know of any. As I paged through the book, I felt hot breath on my elbow.

I turned to see Dudley standing behind me, on his hind legs, appearing to try to decipher the book I had open. He never put a paw on me to balance himself. He didn't need to. I don't know why this freaked me out so much, but it did.

I found myself shrieking at him, "Get down, you little weirdo. You're a quadruped. People stand on two legs, not dogs! This isn't even in the book. It isn't in any book. You're just odd!"

Dudley dropped back down to all four legs. He looked crushed. I felt terrible. He hadn't done anything wrong. *What was wrong with me? Why was I so unnerved? Too little sleep? Too many animals?* It didn't matter. Neither of those things were an excuse to be unkind. He didn't deserve it, not for this anyway. I moved to pat him and apologize. He wouldn't make eye contact with me. My violent outbreak cured that particular habit. He never did it again. I felt awful, and I did deserve it.

On his first trip to the veterinarian, he was a total basket case. He sure wasn't quiet about it, either. I couldn't help thinking of all the times when I sat in the vet's office with my well-behaved German shepherds or lethargic bullmastiffs and clucked derisively at the whacko dogs that were making the mother of all scenes. We had them beat in spades.

Once in the doctor's office, he began filling out the paperwork. Under "breed," he just shook his head and said, "Do you mind if I just put 'canine'?"

I assured him we didn't mind but asked what his best guess would be as to Dudley's breed. He replied that Dudley was obviously mostly border collie and had some pit bull in him, and possibly even an additional breed in the mix. He saw me cringe involuntarily when he said pit bull.

"Don't feel that way. Some dogs that are one hundred percent pit bull make lovely pets."

"I know, but we didn't get him until he was over five months old. I don't think he has been properly socialized, especially around small children. We have three grandchildren. And although he doesn't seem aggressive toward other dogs here, he will not tolerate them in our home."

"Probably afraid he's going to lose the good thing he knows he has going. Doesn't want to lose his place," the vet said kindly. Then he added, "If you still feel nervous as time goes by, we will give you a list of professional dog trainers who we have had experience with and recommend. If it makes you feel better, you can call one of them. If nothing else, they can evaluate him and let you know if they see him as a potential danger."

That did make me feel better, and I was more than happy to take the list.

One of the television shows about dog training strongly suggested daily walks. We tried, but when I took Dudley by myself, I had a terrible time controlling him. If we passed another dog on the street, and the dog strained at his leash, it was all I could do to stop Dudley from pulling the leash out of my hand. Once, when a very large man with two huskies that seemed to be spoiling for a fight approached us, I had to wrap Dudley's leash around the corner stop sign in order to stop him from charging forward. I didn't have the strength to stop him. The man with the huskies marched by, looking at me with contempt, but it was all he could do to control his dogs. Jerk.

I invariably came home with a sore arm and what felt like a dislocated shoulder after these outings. We went to dinner with old friends, and the husband mentioned that he couldn't believe we had gotten another dog. Me either, but our minds were on entirely different tracks.

He said, "You have such great dogs. They're like part of your family. I don't know how you stand it when you lose one. I just don't know how you can handle it."

"I'm not afraid of that with this one, Paul. He's going to live a really, really long life. He may even outlive me."

"How do you know?"

"Because he's just that annoying."

In Dudley's defense, he was probably the smartest and happiest dog we've ever had or ever will have. Maybe he had some sort of species confusion. I'm not sure he knew he was a dog. Besides the standing up on his hind legs thing, he also studied our faces intently whenever we talked to him. And he mimicked our facial expressions. I have heard of that before. Not sure I believed it then, but I do now. His vocabulary was impressive, and it's not because we tried to train him to understand anything but the basic commands. He also made a variety of weird noises in trying to communicate with us. Sometimes I was sorry he couldn't. Sometimes I was grateful.

If I said to Rich, "I have to go to the store," Dudley would wake from a sound sleep and run to the garage door. If you asked him if he would like to take a walk, he got his leash. If we mentioned going out to put the horses in, he rushed to the back door. He recycled all of our plastic bottles by putting them in the recycle bin and brought Rich's clean socks up to his dresser after I took them from the dryer and balled them up. He could also turn the lights on and off. Okay, the last three things I taught him, but his mind and body had to be busy, or he came up with his own stuff. Some we didn't mind; some we did. And he picked things up so quickly it almost seemed a stretch to say I "taught" him.

As far as the happy part goes, he couldn't wait to greet the day, no matter what the weather. I would wake up to see him trotting around the bedroom, sometimes standing up (now he at least leaned) to look out the window at the horses. All the time, his tail was wagging—not frantically, but held high and jaunty with the little white tip bobbing around. He adored the horses, although, sadly, it was an unrequited love. No matter what had happened during day, he was still upbeat at the end of the night. There are not many people (or dogs) you can say that about. There is something to be said for attitude. He was so optimistic he would even break into lazy tail wagging when he was sound asleep. His dreams were happy dreams.

We kind of worked out a little routine. When I worked outside with the horses, he would happily play in the enclosure, as long as he could see me. This also had a weird twist. We tried giving him Luther's stuffed "babies." He immediately tore the stuffing out of them; cotton filling was strewn everywhere.

Then he retrieved the squeaker. At first, I was afraid he would choke on it, but it was a needless worry. He would follow me around with the squeaker in his mouth, making it squeak by squeezing it. When I made a dive to retrieve it, he dashed out of my reach. As soon as I resumed what I was doing, I would hear squeak, squeak, squeak, as he pressed into the back of my knees.

When I finally got it away from him, he was never offered another stuffed toy. Luther was probably rolling over in his grave anyway.

Although he had dozens of toys, his favorite game, the one that kept him happy and busy, was one he had invented himself. It seemed to have some sort of structure or rules involved, but I didn't pretend to know what they were. I don't know if he had a name for it, either, but we called it "Rock."

He would find a rock (not hard in New England) and dig it up. Then he picked it up in his mouth and tossed it in the air. When it landed, he used his two front legs to throw it through his rear legs. If you've ever watched a center in football, you know what I mean. When the rock landed, he twisted around and repeated the process. When he tired of a particular rock, he carried it up the steps and deposited it on our deck. Then he would find another and begin again. A cloud of dust constantly surrounded him.

We almost always had a deck full of rocks, and if I was working in the front yard, he deposited them on our front porch. When there were so many we couldn't help but trip over them, either Rich or I would toss them into the woods. The next day, he would fill them up again. It got so we didn't even notice them.

Sometimes he chose a rock that was too big and heavy for him to lift. He danced around it, whining and looking at me pathetically. He wanted me to help him carry it, and no, I didn't. Believe it or not, even I have my limits. There were a million more rocks he could choose from, and eventually, when he didn't get the assistance he wanted, he would move on.

We were worried that he might break a tooth. I've heard of dogs doing that. I've also heard of rock eaters that end up with rocks in their stomachs and need surgery. His veterinarian checked him. His teeth were perfect, and she didn't feel the need to X-ray his stomach, because she said if he were swallowing rocks, he would have been losing weight. Besides, I think I can account for every rock he'd ever excavated. So his health was perfect. His behavior remained a mystery. Bottom line, he wasn't hurting anything, not even himself, so the game of "Rock" continued.

I should mention that our sunny, funny little dog also had a dark side. We were about to have this brought to our attention in a way that even we couldn't rationalize away.

Chapter 13

The Reckoning

If I took too long in my chores, Dudley simply scrambled over the fence to join me. Sometimes he continued Rock; sometimes he jumped in the fishpond or the horses' water trough. As long as I was there, he never seemed to wander too far. I always kept an eye out, and when I didn't see him, I just called his name, and up popped his little black-and-white face and the white tip of his tail. I couldn't help but think of Lil' Bitty.

That's why I panicked one day when he disappeared. I hadn't even noticed he was gone until I heard this tremendously loud, menacing, bark. I couldn't see Dudley, but the bark was coming from someplace close. All I could think was some huge dog, or coyote, or even wolf was going to eat my little dog. I ran as fast as I could through the woods.

If I had stopped to think about it, even for a minute, I would have had to admit that Dudley wasn't really a "little" dog. Also, anything that could hurt him could certainly do some damage to me. It didn't matter. I ran like a mad woman toward the sound. When I got to the edge of the woods, I saw a dog that looked like Dudley, but much, much bigger. He was barking and growling at something, and the fur was standing up on the back of his neck.

At the sound of my approach, the dog's head swiveled around and looked at me. It was Dudley. I was stunned. As he approached me, he seemed to shrink back to his normal size. The fur on his neck went down, his ears drooped, and his tail went between his legs. He brushed by me on his way home. I looked past the spot he had been standing in and saw my neighbor's front yard. There was a small plastic child's table with half-eaten sandwiches, overturned plastic cups, and small plastic chairs lay askew on the lawn—all the evidence of an interrupted picnic.

"Dudley! What did you do?"

I didn't have a leash on him, and his coming to me was not a given, but something in the tone of my voice registered. He slunk to my side. I stared at him in disbelief.

"What did you do!" I repeated. It wasn't really a question this time; the scene in front of me had my stomach churning.

I could sense a walk of shame coming by this time, but I had no intention of taking this one alone.

I grabbed onto Dudley's collar, and we marched to my neighbor's house. At our approach, the owner, Lillian, and her two small children ventured onto their porch. Her mother followed tentatively behind them.

"You probably think we're silly, but he scared us," she began to explain.

I looked at her two small children. The little girl was about four years old, and the little boy couldn't have been over two. The sounds of the menacing barks and growls rolled around in my head. I felt my heart sink.

"You're not silly," I interrupted. "If it were me, I probably would have called the police." And I meant it.

"Oh, I wouldn't do that. I know he wouldn't really hurt us."

I looked down at Dudley, my hand firmly gripping his collar. He was subdued, but not showing the slightest signs of friendliness, not even with me standing there. I wasn't sure he wouldn't hurt them. My world was upside down. I wasn't sure of anything.

"Can I pat the puppy?" the little girl asked. Her mother and I locked eyes over her head.

"It's pretty hot today, honey, and I think he's a little grumpy. Why don't we come back another time?"

Lillian nodded her head in agreement.

"I'm so terribly sorry. I promise you this will never happen again."

"It's okay, really. My husband will make fun of me for overreacting. Everything is fine."

I nodded and turned to leave. But I didn't think everything was fine. I wasn't sure anything was fine at all. I felt sick to my stomach.

I held on to Dudley's collar until we got into the house. It would be a lie if I said we hadn't seen warning signs before this. Whenever anyone came to our door, he would explode.

I'm pretty sure he single-handedly caused our pizza deliveryman to change occupations. It was already aggravating enough to trek all the way out to our house. Throw Dudley and his hysterics into the mix and I guess it just wasn't worth it.

We made excuses for him; we obfuscated and rationalized. We did this with ourselves and with each other. A lot of dogs act protective when a stranger comes to the door. But Dudley was way over the top. He didn't calm down once someone entered the house, either. We knew he wasn't socialized properly. Because we lived in such a remote area, he wasn't really exposed to other people very often. We have a lot of wonderful friends, but none that I would ask to help calm down an aggressive dog. Maybe that's why we still have friends.

It was our problem, but I really thought it would work out in time and with training. When our children visited, we tried to make him accept them, and them him. He wasn't buying it, and neither were they. I was never afraid of him, and I never for a minute thought he would hurt either Rich or me. However, now the evidence couldn't be ignored. He was getting worse, not better. He had left his property to confront and threaten other people, on their own property.

I sat in the kitchen looking at him. He lay on the floor and looked back. He knew something was up, but he didn't know what. We had never had a dog that was a threat to anyone or anything before. He was openly hostile to other dogs when we went for our walks. At least I had always assumed it was the other dogs. *Was it possible it was the people he didn't like? Could it be that our Dudley was dangerous?* I knew that statistics showed most dog bites involve medium- to large-sized dogs and children under five.

Sometimes the dogs are provoked; sometimes they feel threatened. Sometimes they may have a reason but can't tell us. Sometimes, like some people, I suspect they are just crazy.

Dudley rose from his resting place and slowly approached me. He put his front paws on my lap, leaned up, and licked my cheek. That was the first time I realized tears had begun to fall. I just didn't know what we would do if Dudley did turn out to be an honest-to-God threat. Actually, I did know; that explained the tears. I brushed them away as Dudley began to wriggle his way up onto my lap. This was not something we had ever done before, but we had had a bit of a day, and I made no effort to stop him. I sat in the kitchen chair with a sixty-five-pound dog in my lap, and I held him the way I had held my children when they were small—much smaller than he—but then, his body wasn't in line with his age.

When Rich came home, he could tell just by looking at me that something had gone terribly wrong. I explained about the picnic.

"Is it possible he was trying to herd them? You know, the way he tries with the cats and horses?"

"I don't know. He seemed awfully aggressive. And I've never heard him bark and growl like that before."

"But it's possible?"

"I guess so. But does it matter what his reason was?"

"I guess not. What are we going to do?"

"I don't know. We can't keep him if he's dangerous. And to make matters worse, we can't even keep him on our property. If we return him to the pound—well, I don't think he has another return in him. Remember how anxious he was when we got him? We'd have to tell them about the aggression. What if a family with little kids tried to adopt him? And with all the unwanted friendly dogs out there, I don't think they would even try..." My words hung in the air ominously unfinished.

"Why don't we call one of the dog trainers that the vet suggested? At least that way we can get a professional opinion before we do something we regret."

Did I mention my husband is a handsome fellow? Right then, he looked like a combination of Cary Grant and Robert Redford.

"That's a wonderful idea! I never even thought of that!.

"Calm down," Rich cautioned. "He may tell us something we don't want to hear."

I knew that, but now I had hope. The thing with feathers that perches in the soul—at least according to Emily Dickinson. I just knew it was a wonderful thing, and I hadn't had it until my husband walked through the door.

We called one of the dog trainers and made an appointment for him to come to our house as soon as possible. In the meantime, I made a lasagna for Lillian and her family. It turned out the baby was allergic to tomato sauce. Sometimes you tank even when you're just trying to kiss up. Life can be like that.

I had explained our concerns briefly over the phone to the trainer. He thought he should come to our house to see Dudley in his usual surroundings. I agreed this was a good idea. He also wanted both Rich and me to be there. Another good idea.

He arrived exactly on time, carrying a black satchel. I regret that I don't remember his name. When he rang the bell, Dudley went into his usual hysterics. I opened the door, and Rich restrained our dog. Once inside, without even looking at Dudley, he told us to let him go. He had two good ideas in a row, but it didn't look like the streak would last. He moved to the kitchen and sat down. He motioned for us to take seats as well.

Dudley, once released, charged toward the stranger. Not only didn't he flinch, but he didn't even look at the dog. Dudley began to circle around him, growling ominously. The trainer, whose name I still can't remember, continued to ignore the dog and converse quietly with us. While this was going on, Tommy emerged from under the couch, probably to see what was going on, more likely to check out the new arrival's valuables. This was something I didn't even want to try to explain.

The man ignored Dudley, and Dudley ignored Tommy. We were asked if Dudley and Tommy were left alone together. I explained that we had to leave Dudley in the house because of his ability to climb, so they were together five days a week. On Mondays they were alone for up to ten hours.

"Any problems between them?"

"No."

"Well, that's a good sign."

I felt more hopeful, even though Dudley was circling menacingly around the trainer like the shark in *Jaws*. The trainer opened his satchel, still ignoring Dudley. He didn't take anything out, just left it open. Now he had Dudley's attention in a different way. He stopped acting aggressively; now he was curious.

"There are dog treats in the bag," the trainer explained. "He can smell them. Just ignore him."

So we all did.

"What are your most pressing concerns?"

"Aggression," I said. "I'm afraid he could hurt someone, especially a child."

"Why do you think that?"

"Well, I suspect he might be part pit bull..."

"Doesn't matter."

Okay. That was good.

"And he's acting aggressively." I explained about the walks and the picnic. He already knew firsthand how Dudley acted when confronted with a stranger. "And he's not properly socialized. He was already five months old when we adopted him. I don't know how to do it at this point."

"You may be right. But he's what now, about six months? It's not too late."

Thank God.

Dudley was noticeably calmer, now more curious than anything. And this man hadn't even done anything yet. I took that as a very encouraging sign. The trainer talked on, explaining how he had trained search-and-rescue dogs and telling us stories about some of the dogs he had confronted. This was not boring at all; it was soothing. He talked softly and calmly. It seemed like the house itself exhaled and relaxed. Then he got down to business.

"After observing you and your husband," he began.

Lord, I didn't know he was observing us. If I had, I might have sat up a little straighter or something.

"It appears to me that you are both pretty easygoing people. Is that right?"

We both shook our heads in affirmation.

"And," he continued, looking at Rich, "I feel that when you do say no, you mean no. Is that right?"

Rich agreed it was.

Looking at me, he said, "And when you say no, you mean maybe. Is that right?"

Okay, I wasn't happy about that remark, but he wasn't wrong. I owned up to my own wishy-washiness; there was too much at stake here to dissemble. This could be Dudley's only chance. I nodded in agreement.

"Who has the majority of dog responsibilities?'

"Well, it's Rich's dog. He got Dudley for his birthday. It was his idea."

This was met by silence.

"But…"

More silence. This man shouldn't be a dog trainer; he should be interrogating people for the FBI. He had me spilling my guts, with no apparent effort on his part.

"Well," I continued. I had to fill that silence. "Rich works from eight to ten hours a day, and I work part time. So I guess you would say he's my responsibility the majority of the time."

"Okay, good. A couple of things right up front. You have other animals, I can see that. I suspect you always have. You seem very comfortable around all of them, even the dog you're concerned about. You've had other dogs before, right?"

More nodding on our parts.

"But you've never had one like Dudley?"

I was tempted to say, *There are no other dogs like Dudley*, but bit my tongue and just agreed yet another time.

"Do you know what breeds your other dogs were?"

We told him about the German shepherds and the bullmastiffs.

"Well then," he smiled slightly, "I can see why Dudley was quite a surprise for you. I can't tell you for sure what breeds comprise Dudley, but the most dominant one is border collie. The thing about border collies is that they are extremely smart, possibly the smartest breed. However, they also have a highly developed work ethic, and their chase and herding instincts are very strong. They have a tremendous amount of energy. They were bred to herd sheep day and night over rocky, hostile terrain. They have extraordinary endurance. "

Okay, so far he hadn't said anything about a maul or kill instinct. I was also glad we hadn't made more of an issue about Dudley's sleeping arrangements. This didn't sound like a dog we could outlast in the long run.

I liked this man, and I was trying to take in every word, but I couldn't help noticing Tommy jump into his open satchel. Rich pulled Tommy out, and he jumped back in again. We removed him once again and secured him in the bathroom. The trainer smiled and said he could probably smell the treats. He may know dogs, but he didn't know Tommy. It was more likely Tommy was looking for a Rolex.

Dudley was now sitting by the trainer's side, getting his ears ruffled. They were like old buddies. I really didn't know what we had signed up for. *Would there be lessons? Would they be expensive? Would they be every day or once a week and for how long?* I was about to find out.

"The most important thing for any dog is leadership."

I couldn't help noticing he was looking at me when he said this. Apparently, Rich was a natural leader. Me, not so much. But I was willing to work at it.

"The quickest way to establish leadership in a pack—and dogs are pack animals—is lots and lots of long walks."

God, kill me now, just the thought of it and my shoulder was starting to throb. He couldn't have missed the wince I made.

"Walks aren't fun?"

You can add comedian to his résumé.

"Don't worry, that's an easy fix."

Really? That hadn't been my experience.

"Have you ever heard of a Gentle Leader?"

Annie had mentioned them, but said it was better if you had a professional show you how to use it. Okay, we had the professional; bring on the Gentle Leader. And he did. He pulled a nylon leash out of his case. It was attached to what looked like a nylon halter for a very small horse. It had a loop that went over the dog's nose, but didn't stop him from panting or barking—or biting. It had another nylon strap that went around the dog's head and fastened behind his ears. The leash was attached to a metal ring under the dog's chin.

"It's a lot like the halters you use for your horses. Control the head and you control the animal."

I didn't have the nerve to say that that hadn't been entirely our experience with the horses, and in truth, it did work most of the time.

He put the leader on Dudley, and we went outside. Dudley immediately tried to rub it off on the ground. The trainer ignored him and just pulled him along. And he went. He was controlling Dudley using just two fingers on the leash. Next, one at a time, he had both Rich and me walk up and down the street with the dog. Dudley was now paying attention to us and trotting along. A man and his dog passed, going in the opposite direction. The dog barked at Dudley. Dudley never even looked at him. *Is this a magic leash?* I couldn't believe it. There was no pain for us, and it certainly didn't look like it was hurting the dog.

The trainer gave us more tips about controlling Dudley when people entered the house, but said we might not want to stop him from barking at strangers completely. No problem, even with his tips, we were never able to pull that off. He then told us to make sure we did our homework and he would come back in about two weeks.

"Is Dudley dangerous?" I asked.

"We'll talk in a couple of weeks. But in my experience, most people with problem dogs turn out to be dogs with problem people."

I never in my life took a homework assignment so seriously. Dudley and I marched up and down the street and around the block several times a day. Rich pitched in whenever he had some free time. I'm not going to tell you it was an instantaneous fix. It wasn't. It took a lot of walks and a lot of time, and more than four years later, we were still working on some things. But what I do know for sure is we wouldn't have known what direction to go in if it weren't for the dog trainer.

Approximately two weeks later, we got a call from the trainer saying he was on his way to our house. He told us to be outside with Dudley and said he wouldn't be coming to the door. Okay, this was interesting. Rich and I stood in the front yard with Dudley on his leash, or I should say "Gentle Leader." Suddenly, from the woods, we could hear a lot of thrashing and shouting. Dudley was on red alert, but the leader stopped him from charging. He stood between us and the noise. The trainer came out of the woods, still shouting and banging a large stick into nearby trees. Dudley held his ground.

When the man got to within a few feet of us, he dropped the stick and smiled. He looked down at Dudley and said, "How are you doing, buddy?"

Dudley wagged his tail tentatively.

"Good dog!"

By now, all four of us were beaming like morons. I'm including Dudley; his smile was always one of his best things. It's why we got him.

"Did you notice how he placed himself between you and what he perceived as danger?"

Actually, I hadn't until he mentioned it, but it was a good point.

"He is a good dog. I don't believe he is dangerous by nature. But you do have to be strong leaders. Both of you. If he senses a leadership vacuum, he'll step right in. But he obviously loves you and wants to please. He's made a huge improvement. Just keep working with him, and of course, never leave any dog alone with a child."

"How do we keep him on our property? You know, if he sees a deer or rabbit or something."

"Do you have any objection to electronic fences?"

We assured him we didn't.

"Then get one. Still don't leave him outside alone. I've told you about his chase instinct; the fence alone may not stop him. Combine it with his respect for you, and that will probably do the trick."

"When will you be coming back?"

"I won't be. You are conscientious people with a nice dog. You have all the tools you need. If you run into any problems, feel free to call me. Otherwise, I think you'll all be fine."

We were desperate when we called him, and we were paying by the visit. He could have dragged this out until it cost us a fortune. And we would have gone along for as long as we thought it would help Dudley. This trainer didn't do that to us. He could have. We weren't the only ones who were conscientious. For the first time since we had brought Dudley home, my mind and heart were at ease about him. Just in time for the horses to throw us a curve.

Chapter 14
Showdown

Since we were admittedly new to the horse world, we found just watching Raz and Penny interact was more interesting than television. We had built the barn directly behind the house, and the attached paddock could easily be seen from our kitchen. The whole "dominant" thing had taken us by surprise, and we liked to watch it play out. Even after establishing she was the boss, Raz would occasionally sashay over to Penny and flatten her ears back. Penny dutifully moved off. She never went far, never seemed to put much effort into it, and did not seem particularly intimidated. At least not to me, and I knew her pretty well.

The two of them liked to play together, and we would watch them line up beside each other and then race to the opposite end of the field. Both of them were very fast and competitive. They also loved chasing each other around, running and bucking for all they were worth. But they no longer kicked out at each other.

Once, when riding back to the barn, Rich and I inadvertently lined up side by side. Before you could say, "I'd really rather be reading," we were off to the races on a short, narrow dirt path that was barely two horses wide. It got worse because it got even narrower as we approached the barn, which we were doing at breakneck speed. Pun reluctantly intended. The paddock gate had been left open, and I was able to steer Penny to the right, into the paddock. Rich and Raz whipped around the back of the barn. Stopping them would have been our preference, but it didn't seem to be an option. We were careful not to set up that scenario again. However, we enjoyed watching them, as long as we weren't on board and their surroundings were relatively safe.

They had two distinctly different personalities. I think their main personality difference can be summed up in one sentence. Penny loved us; Raz loved Penny. Penny was very people-oriented, and if left in a field to graze, alone or with Raz, all you usually needed to do was whistle and she came. Even if she didn't want to leave and wouldn't come, she would stand quietly while you approached her. Then you could just put a hand on her halter and lead her away. No fuss, no muss.

Raz was all fuss and muss, making even the simplest chore a challenge. She would never come to you, and if you approached her, it became a game of "catch me if you can." If left alone to graze with Penny, we could never catch her. After a while, we ceased trying. We found all we had to do was remove Penny, and Raz panicked. We would stroll away with Penny between us and, all of a sudden, would hear galloping hooves behind us. Raz would come screeching up, terrified that Penny was leaving her alone.

That was part of what confused me about the dominance issue. I knew from the beginning Penny would not be easy to push around. However, she was battling chronic lameness, the root cause of which we still didn't know. She had good stretches and bad stretches. During a good stretch, we would take them on trail rides. If we separated to explore different paths, it was only a matter of minutes until Raz came galloping up to be with Penny. Rich used all his knowledge and strength to dissuade her, and by this time, he had a fair share of both. He still couldn't stop Raz from rejoining Penny. I wouldn't have had a snowball's chance in hell.

Although both horses were high strung, Penny was braver than Raz, forging through water, unfamiliar territory, and if she spooked, either Rich or I could bring her under control. Raz only felt safe if Penny was calm. From what we could tell, her trust in us was around zero. If they had to be separated for some reason, Raz would call out constantly night and day. I lived in fear of coming home from work and being greeted by the ASPCA. It was understandable that someone would call about a horse in distress. I can't imagine what people thought we were doing to her to make her cry out like that. It was a pathetic and relentless sound. Thankfully, no one ever complained about the noise.

On the other hand, if Raz had to be removed for a day or two, Penny barely looked up. She had us, which was fine with her. You could hear Raz calling her from the horse trailer as it pulled away. It was kind of sad and more than a little confusing. This didn't strike me as the way a boss would act toward a subservient. But then, horses are weird people. On occasion,

Raz would exert her dominance, just to make sure Penny understood who was in charge. One day, we hauled them up to Becca's, where we were all going on a trail ride. Raz kicked Penny in a hind leg while in the trailer. We didn't know it until we unloaded them and saw the blood running down Penny's leg.

Luckily, Becca was able to Steri-Strip the wound, and we didn't have to try to find a veterinarian on a Saturday. Becca did a fine job, but there would be no trail riding that day. Up until this incident, Raz had just used occasional intimidation, the showing of teeth or flattening of ears. I don't know what caused this escalation, but it made me nervous. When it comes to drawing blood, both Rich and I are kind of candy asses.

We decided that if the horses were left alone, one would be locked in her stall, and the other would have the run of the paddock. When I got home from work, I just switched them out so they both had the same amount of exercise time.

This seems like a mild change, but it set up a whole new set of circumstances that left us wondering if we had lost our minds. I mean, more than usual.

The first thing that had us going was coming home and finding Raz in the paddock with no halter on. The halter wasn't missing. It would be lying in the dirt someplace. When Penny was being boarded, we got into trouble because we were accused of taking her halter off at night. This was against their rules. We didn't agree with the rule, but were on shaky ground anyway, so we weren't about to violate it.

Most of these halters can be fastened in two ways: One is with a metal clasp at the side of the horse's face; the second is by unbuckling it on the side. Rich and I invariably used the metal clasp because it was easier and faster. Penny's halter, when found in her stall, wasn't undone at all. By stealthy observation, we watched her duck her head under a triangular-shaped food dish. She would catch the brow band on the rim and then back out.

We had the halter on too loose. We really didn't like using one in the stall at all, but our loosening it allowed her to remove it. We tightened it up, and that solved the problem until we took her home. Then we never had a halter on either horse while they were in their stalls. However, and they learned this pretty quickly, they never left the stall without one. A loose horse with nothing on it can be almost impossible to catch and hold on to. Don't kid yourself, they all know it. It's a phenomenon Rich and I call bare-naked horse syndrome. People who have ever had to chase down a "naked" horse understand what I mean.

I don't think the halter bothered Penny at all. She was just bored. A bored Penny was a thinking Penny, and that was the result. However, it wasn't Penny that was turning up without a halter. It was Raz. And the halter was undone. The buckle on the side was unbuckled. This only happened when Raz was outside and Penny was locked in.

We tried to figure out what was happening. First, we blamed each other. I mean, that's what married people do. However, it didn't make any sense. We wondered if someone else was coming in and taking off Raz's halter and throwing it in the dirt. That didn't make any sense, either. What would be the point? And even more telling, Raz was not a horse that could be easily approached by a stranger. She wouldn't stand still for it. Heck, sometimes she wouldn't stand still for us. After this had happened more than a few times, I happened to have a day off from work. I had put Raz out, and Penny was in her stall. Penny had her head hanging out the open top half of the door. I was doing laundry when I saw Raz walk over to Penny. I stopped what I was doing to watch. Was there going to be a confrontation of some sort?

Both horses stood nose to nose for a couple of minutes. Then Raz turned her head to the side. Penny grasped the halter strap with her teeth. She grasped it above the buckle. Razzy dropped her head, causing the buckle to pop open. Penny let go, and Raz backed up and shook her head. The halter went flying, and Raz went back to munching on her hay. Penny did the same.

I know that horses are not supposed to be that smart. I know they are certainly not supposed to cooperate on tasks. They don't have the higher mentality needed for activities of that nature. This would take cognitive thought. Horses don't have that, or they're not supposed to. All I can say is they did it. I saw it. And I put the halter back on Raz so Rich could see it, too. And he did.

That ended that mystery, but they weren't done screwing with us yet.

Rich took care of the horses in the morning before work. He was managing a machine shop. I had an office job, so it seemed logical. Then, one day, I came home to see both horses in the paddock calmly eating hay. Both doors were wide open. My stomach dropped as I ran to them to see if there were any new cuts or bruises. There weren't. They apparently hadn't been fighting. But they could have been. When Rich came home from work, I lit into him.

"You left Penny's stall open, and both horses were together. For Christ's sake, Rich, they could have killed each other!"

"I didn't leave it open. I always check. And don't overreact. They wouldn't have killed each other." At least that's what we thought then.

"It was open when I got home, and the horses were together. Did you maybe not lock it and Penny pushed it open?"

"No, I checked the lock. I always do."

"Are you sure?"

"Absolutely!"

"How did it get open?"

"I don't know. I'm almost positive I locked it."

"Almost?"

"No, dammit, I'm positive! Don't do that. I'm not that sure of myself, so I check it every day."

In Rich's defense, I will say they we were both aware that we were getting older. The fact that we were forgetting things seemed glaring, probably no more than before, but as you age, you lose your confidence. You start to question yourself more. So we had both taken to double-checking anything we thought important. We both thought this was important.

"If you're sure you locked it, how did it get open?"

"Maybe somebody came by while we were at work and opened it?"

"Seriously, you want to go down that path again?"

"What do you mean?"

"I mean the same as with the halter. We were blaming some mysterious stranger when all the time it was the horses themselves."

We looked at each other and shut up for a minute.

Then Rich said, "Put Penny in and Raz out."

"I just swapped them. It's Penny's turn to be out."

"Just do it."

I did, and we sat to watch. In the interest of full disclosure, I will say that I poured myself a glass of wine. I got Rich a beer. If this was going the way I suspected it would, I would have preferred something stronger. Sure enough, I had just returned to the house when Penny stuck her head out. She was working her lips down the side of the door.

"I don't believe it," Rich said. "That's a slide bolt; she'll never be able to open it."

She did. And then she walked out and joined Raz.

As crazy-making as these incidents were, we couldn't help feeling at least a little good about them. Penny had been going through an unusually protracted period of soundness. We could see it when we rode her. Lameness didn't seem to be an issue. Now with her up to her old tricks, we had to believe she was going in the right direction. When Penny was feeling good, she invariably was making mischief.

The farrier who had helped her confirmed our belief. The day he came to shoe her, he watched her move—walk, jog, and lope, the three gaits most commonly used with horses. Penny, being Penny, threw in a full-blown gallop just for the heck of it. She wasn't asked to. But no one could have stopped her.

The farrier couldn't help himself; he laughed, and then he said, "I didn't think she'd ever be one hundred percent again. Looks like I was wrong."

That was something we could all be happy about. He left, and I put Penny back in her stall. I let Raz out and gave her some hay. Then I had a brainstorm. *Why not let them back together?* They were obviously getting along better, cooperating with each other, and generally bonding. I would be standing right there, what could happen? I opened Penny's door. She was happy and playful. I kept a wary eye on Raz, but she didn't seem to care one way or the other. Penny stepped into the paddock and swung her head around and looked at Raz. Then Penny headed for Raz like a guided missile.

Raz saw her coming and swung her hindquarters around. They both screamed—a rage-filled, horrid noise that made the hair stand up on the back of my neck. Penny swung around so her hindquarters were positioned behind Raz's. Then they commenced to kicking the crap out of each other. I had never seen anything like it. Not even in the movies. I hastily stepped into Penny's stall and closed the bottom part of the door. I didn't know what to do.

Then I heard the scuffle of toenails on concrete and caught sight of Dudley rushing past me. I grabbed him just as he launched himself at the door.

"Seriously? You're going to straighten this out?" I couldn't fault his intentions or his courage. He obviously had more than I did. Plus, I didn't have a clue as to my next move. The only thing I was sure of was I couldn't let him in the middle of it. Rich was expected home in about an hour. We might be down one horse, maybe two. I wasn't about to lose Dudley as well. I took a lead rope and snapped it on his collar, tying him inside the barn.

This was only minutes, but it seemed much longer. And the horses seemed to be ramping up rather than tiring out. They stood like two flat-footed boxers and just kept hammering at each other. I knew I needed to do something. And fast.

I tried yelling, "Whoa!" but, honestly, it might have come out a shaky "Whoa?" It didn't matter. I don't think they heard me, and if they did, they ignored me. Their eyes were glazed. They seemed to have tunnel vision. They were focusing only on each other and each other's destruction. They never stopped screaming, and their ears were flattened back against their heads, their faces distorted. It was ugly.

I tried distracting them by pounding on a metal bucket with a stick. Again, I was ignored. I threw the bucket near them, not at them. It landed with a clang, right under them. Nothing changed. It was past feeding time, but I couldn't imagine that would make a difference. However, nothing else came to mind. I poured grain in their buckets. They both stopped at the same time.

They swung their heads around and looked at me as if to ask, "Supper?"

"Uh, yeah."

"Okay, we'll eat; then we'll kill each other." They marched into their respective stalls.

I shot around front and locked them in. My hands were shaking so badly I could barely lock the doors. How the hell had Penny worked that lock with her mouth? I untied Dudley and put him in the house, where I knew he would be safe. My next job would be to check the horses and see if they needed medical attention. Frankly, I didn't want to go near either one of them. My brain was still processing what I had seen and heard. I was torn between disbelief and fear. I took several deep breaths and waited until I stopped shaking. I couldn't put it off any longer; one or both of them could be seriously hurt. Even though Penny started it, I assumed she got the worst of it. She was smaller than Raz; that couldn't help. Also, I felt less afraid of her than Raz, but only a little at this point.

I entered Penny's stall as she contentedly downed the grain in her bucket. She calmly turned her head to look at me. Her eyes were calm and soft and innocent looking. She seemed glad to see me. *Where was that demon from hell I had locked in the stall?* I tied her and started to run my hands over her body, looking for damage. I couldn't help noticing that my hands had begun to tremble again.

I did a fairly thorough examination, and I couldn't find any signs of the fight. There was probably swelling; I wouldn't have been able to determine that. However, I knew nothing was broken, and amazingly, there was no blood. *How was that possible?* Both horses had shoes on their front feet, but we had declined to put them on the rear. Just in case. *Still, how could she survive that pounding unscathed?* Maybe my mind exaggerated what had happened. I hoped so.

I untied Penny and moved on to Raz. I was well aware that I did not have the same relationship with Razzy that I had with Penny—or the relationship I thought I had with Penny. I no longer knew where any of us stood.

My mind flashed back to an incident that had taken place shortly after we got Raz. I brought her back from the round pen, where she had been grazing. While I was leading her, I noticed one of her eyes was swollen shut. This didn't alarm me much. It is pretty common with horses. It could have been as simple as a bug bite. But I am a mother, and I felt bad for her. I put her in her stall and secured her with crossties. This involves two ropes, one on each side, attached to the wall and then attached to the horse's halter. We had equipped both stalls with crossties. This makes handling horses safer. At least that's what it's supposed to do.

After I had her secured, I went into the house to get ice. I wrapped the ice in a towel. My intention was to place it on the affected eye and reduce the swelling. I had left the door to the stall open to the paddock. Raz was in crossties and wasn't going anywhere. I approached her with my makeshift icepack. Her head shot up. I could understand her being nervous; she didn't know my intentions. Also, she hadn't known me for long. I was sure that once she felt the cool ice on her face, we would both be fine. I'll never know. When I tried to place the ice on her elevated face, I saw the whites of her eyes. Then she reared back with all her strength and power and snapped the ropes of the crossties like they were string. She bolted into the paddock, knocking me over in the process. The next day, her eye was fine, but we had to replace the crossties.

This is what I was thinking about when I entered her stall. The door stayed firmly shut. I put her in the crossties, but it didn't give me much of a feeling of security. She was subdued, and it was easy to tie her. I started to run my hands over her hindquarters. Within seconds, they were wet and sticky. It was blood. There was a fair amount of it, too. Because of the sweat, it was hard to tell exactly where it was coming from, but it was both hind legs.

I had brought towels with me. Although I couldn't help remembering my prior attempt to nurse her, I knew I had to try to stop the bleeding. I wet a towel and used it to clean up the area. She had several lacerations on her hind legs. One of her legs was bleeding pretty badly. It wasn't spurting, so I knew it wasn't an artery. I folded the towel and pressed it against the deepest wound. Raz leaned back into the pressure. It was like she knew I was trying to help her. For a second, I mused at how far we had come, she and I. Then I remembered the fight and decided I didn't know anything at all about either horse.

We stayed that way until the bleeding slowed and then stopped. Rich came home from work. I told him what had happened or tried to. I handed him the towel. I told him to call the vet if he thought Raz needed to be seen. I told him I had something I had to do. And I did. I went in the house and threw up.

Chapter 15
Aftermath

Raz's wounds were relatively superficial. The one I had put pressure on had already stopped bleeding. It didn't seem necessary to call the vet. We added a topical antibiotic and just agreed to watch her healing carefully. Without even discussing it, Rich drove two additional poles in the ground. He ran two strands of electrical tape between them, effectively cutting the paddock in two. That way both horses could be let out at the same time and not be able to hurt each other. They could still interact with each other over the fence. And they would have the freedom to go in and out of their own stalls as they wished.

Their aggression never surfaced when they were being ridden, so that was a big plus. They could also graze peacefully together in a field. That I didn't and still don't understand. Still, the fight shook our faith in both of them. We asked anyone and everyone with any kind of horse experience why they thought the fight had happened. Amazingly, the only thing most people were surprised at was the fact that the horses had gotten along for over a year, and then the fight broke out. No one seemed unsettled by the viciousness of it. A lot of people just shook their heads and said, "Yeah, that can happen." Color me surprised.

We heard a lot of theories, and the most prevalent one was the fact that they were both mares. With mares, you are dealing with all the instinct stuff, and then you have to throw in hormones. Having been female my entire life, I had personally experienced the havoc hormones can wreak. Although, in my defense, I've never kicked anyone. But I've wanted to. We were also told that red horses tend to be high strung. Both of ours were a deep chestnut red. It was possible that we had two dominant mares, and Penny was looking to move up in the pecking order. It was also possible that Penny was harboring a grudge about the kick she received in the trailer. That was Becca's thought. And, of course, it could have been all, or none, of the above.

I had my own theory, and it's unfortunate that it hadn't occurred to me until after the fact. Although Raz was larger and a bit older, I was surprised when Penny didn't emerge as dominant in the first place. I don't know how much she would have pushed Raz around; she was pretty people-oriented. But she didn't like being on the receiving end. I had picked up on that when we first introduced them to each other. When she backed off from Raz, she never seemed cowed. She moved when forced to. She never went far or moved fast. It was like she was giving the least possible effort to keep the peace.

In my opinion, the only reason she knuckled under in the first place was because she was still healing. She was dogged by lameness, and it was impossible to tell how much pain she was in. Horses instinctively try to hide disability and pain. It is hardwired into prey animals.

Predators zero in on the old, weak, sick, or disabled. However, once Penny was back to her old self, she asserted her position. This is just my opinion, of course, and I could be way off. Still, the timing seems to bear me out. Also, Raz's dependence on Penny and her extreme attachment to her didn't seem to track with Raz calling the shots. At any rate, it was what it was, and we couldn't change it. We could only try to make sure they were not in a situation where they had the opportunity to turn on each other.

Although both Rich and I were shaken by the fight, each following uneventful day helped it fade a bit from our mutual consciousness. Neither of us would ever forget it, but it seemed less important and horrifying as time passed peacefully. They were horses, after all, and this behavior was not exactly unique to these two, even if it was new to us. If you love something, you take the bad with the good, and that is what we did. We just tried to make sure that another fight wouldn't or couldn't break out on our watch. It never did.

Once the horses were effectively separated from each other, it changed the dynamics of our own personal "herd" once again. Although we were a ragtag interspecies group, a hodgepodge of prey and predators, in the eyes of the animals, we apparently all belonged together. I thought so, too. Not having quite as much contact with Penny, Raz began to interact with us more. Penny, who was already as friendly as a puppy toward people, began to take an interest in Dudley. She had already stopped trying to kill him, and now she sniffed and licked him on occasion. Although Raz was coming around, she wasn't about to go that far.

One day, when I was out cleaning the paddock with my wheelbarrow, Dudley once again climbed the fence to join me. I was on Raz's side of the electric fence, and I didn't think he would venture that far. He didn't. He romped around with Penny for a bit, but then she went back to eating hay. He found a rock and went into his insane, rock-loving, frantic digging. There was a cloud of dust surrounding him as sand flew in all directions. He whined happily in anticipation. All this activity couldn't help but catch Penny's attention.

She swung her head around to watch him, while slowly chewing a mouthful of hay. Finally, her curiosity got the better of her, and she started to amble toward him. He was so engrossed he never saw her coming. I didn't think she would hurt him, but understandably, I was never positive of anything when it came to the horses.

"Dudley," I called out, "pay attention."

He either didn't hear me or ignored me—I could never tell. Penny was still moving toward him.

"Dudley!" I shouted louder this time. "Look out!"

He didn't, and she was almost on top of him. I had started toward them, but Penny wasn't showing any signs of aggression. Her ears were up and tilted forward inquisitively. She was moving slowly and deliberately, so even though I wouldn't make it in time, I felt things would be okay.

By the time Dudley looked up, she was standing directly over him. From his perspective, it must have looked liked a giant floating head. He was standing with one front leg on each side of his hole. He froze in that position, only his eyes darting furtively. It was so easy to read his mind and his body language. He was scared and rightfully so. He wanted to run away. But if he did, *she* could take *his* rock. He stood his ground, bless his courageous little heart. Penny moved slightly to look over him into the hole, as if to say, "Ah, dude, it's a rock."

Once that was established, Penny lost interest and turned to move back to her hay pile. She hadn't taken two steps when Dudley reached into the hole and grabbed his rock. A black-and-white streak shot out of the paddock, rock firmly locked in its jaws. The rocks were never allowed in the house, of course; it was bad enough that they were all over the deck and porch. However, I did let him keep this very special one in the garage. It would have taken a harder heart than I had to take it away from him.

Chapter 16
Interlude

Once our new "herd" was established, things settled down to a relatively uneventful routine. In the late afternoon, I would lead Penny to the round pen to graze. Rich would follow closely behind with Raz. Dudley would scamper in between, occasionally jumping at the horses. Tommy brought up the rear, at a respectful distance. Our very own freak parade of sorts.

Cooter declined to join us. He stayed in the house sulking. The only one he really seemed to like was Tommy. He didn't know how to open the screen, but he slipped quickly out behind Tommy once it was opened. He never ventured out without Tommy. He declined to join him when the rest of us were involved. Since he was always the one following when the cats attempted an escape, I made the mistake of grabbing him in midflight. This only happened a couple of times. Each time he bit me. Hard. The last time he bit and scratched, I ended up at the doctor with IV antibiotics for an infected cat bite. He had all his shots, but any cat bite can become infected. As usual, I learned this the hard way.

If he had been my cat, I'm sure I would have tried to find him a new home. Not that it would have been easy. However, he belonged to our daughter, and I had promised her I would take care of him and try to keep him indoors. I honestly tried. After that last bite, however, when I reached for him on his way out, he rolled onto his back, both teeth and claws at the ready. I backed off and let him go. I should have contacted Annie then and told her I couldn't handle him any longer. But I didn't, and I'm sorry I didn't. It never seemed the right time, or something that seemed more important took precedence. I also rationalized that as long as he was with Tommy, he would be fine. I was wrong.

One afternoon, when I was coming down from the second floor, I heard the screen slide open. Some women living in isolated areas may have thought they had an intruder trying to get in. I knew I had cats that were getting out. By the time I got to the door, all I saw were their respective tails disappear into the woods. Chasing them would be a fool's errand, and I fully expected them both to return. I was only half right. Tommy showed up in time for dinner; however, he was alone. I thought they may have gotten separated in the woods and Cooter would be along later. Tommy didn't seem ruffled or upset in the least. By the next day, we knew Cooter wouldn't be coming back. We began our search and notified the dog officer. Again.

He told us not to get our hopes up. We sent him a picture, as we had for Bitty, but this time, we really didn't think we could reasonably expect a happy ending, not where we live. I was struck with the guilt that you always feel when you let someone down, especially your own child. I dreaded coming clean, but I had to. Cooter clearly wasn't coming home. Tommy would live with us for at least another four years, going in and out at will. Eventually, he came to the same fate as the other cats. At least that seemed a rational assumption. We never even contacted the authorities. We knew Tommy. He was a tough little nut, not easily cracked. If he could come home, he would. I still miss the quirky little thief. Rich and I made a pact to never have another cat where we live. And we never have.

Chapter 17
Penny's Problem

We purchased Penny on June 20, 2004. It's easy to remember because it was Rich's birthday, Father's Day, and they were loading her up to ship her God knows where. Our decision was forced; however, I can't deny that we had pretty much made up our minds. We had been riding her all winter, and we had both fallen in love with her.

It's not like we didn't know the downside. We knew her bad habits, but didn't believe she was a bad or mean horse. We felt all of the negatives could be reversed with the proper amount of love and care. And they were. We also knew about her bouts with lameness; however, lameness is pretty common in horses and can be caused by all kinds of things. We thought one of Penny's problems was that she just wasn't allowed enough exercise.

It didn't seem natural to keep a young horse, full of energy, in a stall for all but an hour or so a week. She may have had other problems, too, such as bad shoeing or abscesses.

We felt this could be reversed as well, with the proper care. In this, we were stunningly wrong.

Penny's problem was navicular syndrome. This is a progressive and incurable condition. There is no proven cause, and diagnosis is usually done by ruling out other causes of lameness. It has a history of slow onset of front limb lameness, and it is not uncommon for a navicular horse to go through protracted periods of seeming soundness, as Penny did.

In fairness to everyone involved, from the people who sold her to us to the veterinarians involved and the stable that she was boarded at, navicular is not easy to diagnose. I doubt any of us really knew what we were dealing with. The others, with more knowledge and experience, may have had their suspicions, but I really don't think anyone *knew* for sure. The truth is we would have bought her anyway.

We didn't have a definite diagnosis until August 8, 2007, when we had Penny evaluated at a hospital for large animals. We were lucky to live within driving distance of a prestigious and well-equipped facility. That is where our luck, and Penny's, ran out.

We brought her there because she had been suffering setbacks more and more frequently, and it took longer for her to recover. Now she appeared lame in all four legs. We had our local veterinarians evaluate her, as well as the farrier who had been helping her. Our veterinarians raised the specter of navicular for the first time, but they couldn't be sure. Also, the only course of action they advised was a bilateral neurectomy, also known as "nerving" a horse. This involves surgically severing the nerves in both front legs so the horse is no longer in pain. Our farrier told us he didn't think he could help her any longer.

We made an appointment with the hospital and trailered Penny to a neighboring state. They X-rayed both front feet and found radiographic changes consistent with navicular in both. They went on to do nerve blocks and determined the problems with her back legs were caused by her shifting all her weight to the rear, in an effort to alleviate the pain in her front legs. Normally, a horse carries 60 percent of its weight in the front because of their large heads, necks, and chests. Shifting that weight to the hind legs would understandably put a tremendous and unnatural strain on them.

They suggested that they keep Penny hospitalized overnight so they could anesthetize her and do a total bone scan. We agreed. A lot was on the line.

When we returned to collect her, we were given the devastating diagnosis. The veterinarian who told us also seemed (at least to me) rather cheerful in their assessment that Penny had the worst case of navicular they had ever seen. I don't think this particular veterinarian thought the diagnosis was as dire as we did. As a matter of fact, I know he didn't, because when I asked if Penny should be euthanized, he looked shocked.

In their written report, Penny was described as being bright and alert. And of course she was. I could have also added smart and funny and incredibly lovable. However, that didn't change the fact that she was in pain, and no one even suggested that it was not going to get much, much worse. She didn't deserve that. I loved her. I didn't want to kill her. When we received her diagnosis, I think I literally felt my heart break. I didn't mean I was thinking about euthanizing her then.

I preferred not to think of it at all. It just seemed that this was where things were leading—at least if we were going to be humane. The vet countered with the fact that she was still very young. He told me to look at the horse in the stall next to her. This animal stood, head hanging, breathing laboriously and staring vacantly. I had assumed when I saw him that he was about a hundred years old. The vet told me he was younger than Penny. I had to admit that, next to him, Penny seemed the picture of health.

The patient care instructions were to continue with the shoes and pads we had already been using and administer pain medication for seven days. She was also to have restricted exercise for four weeks. After that, we could start riding her again. If no improvement was seen, they only offered us one option—a bilateral neurectomy.

People's opinion of this option varies, but each horse is different, and we had special, and I believe valid, reasons to be against it. For one thing, Penny loved to run; she lived for it. She hated restricted exercise. She wouldn't tolerate "stall rest," something some other horses actually seem to luxuriate in. Remove the pain and she would be careening all over the place. That could cause a fatal and horrific breakdown in a horse with diseased legs. Other than the disease, she was her own worst enemy. You never had to encourage Penny to move; you just had to hold her back. We had seen her go from dead lame to racing around, bucking and kicking. That was without pain medication, never mind surgery.

Also, this surgery is temporary. The nerves often reconnect themselves in as little as a year to eighteen months. Then surgery would have to be done all over again. Even without the downsides of the surgery itself, it is only a temporary solution. Nothing changes the fact that navicular is a progressive disease and no matter what was done would relentlessly get more and more severe. I took a big gulp of air to steady myself and thanked them for their help. They had been helpful. Like it or not, at least now we knew for sure what we were dealing with. It might not have been the answer we were praying for, but neither Rich nor I ever doubted for a minute the accuracy of it.

We returned home and followed our instructions to the letter. Penny's back legs had shown immediate improvement. It was hard to tell about the front because we were doing our best to keep her quiet and rest them. We gave her the pain medication, and she immediately felt relief and, in the process, became harder to handle. She wanted to *move*.

After the prescribed four weeks, we decided to take a slow walk around our property. Penny was thrilled. When I rode her into the front yard, she bolted, going at top speed into the woods. I really thought her intention was to jump the stone wall that encircled our property. I was afraid. I was afraid for her. I was terrified for myself.

I wasn't wearing a helmet. I usually don't wear a helmet anyway, but I usually don't ride on pavement, either. I pictured my brains splattered over the road, like a smashed watermelon. I used all my strength to turn her away from the road. I put her in a tight circle by pulling on one rein and kicking her as hard as I could on that side. She fought me every inch of the way, and expletives flew loudly from my mouth. Some words I had never used before. Terror can do that to you. But Penny did circle and stop. I headed her out of the woods, back toward the barn. I intended to walk her slowly. Although she did not make a second attempt to bolt, she pranced all the way back. She was happy as could be. This was the best day she had had in a month. Her neck was arched prettily, and she high-stepped jauntily until she was again in her stall.

A couple of days later, my neighbor from across the street said, "Oh, I saw you riding your horse the other day."

She must have seen Penny out of control and heard me swearing like a longshoreman. I'm not often struck speechless, but I was this time. *What could I say? How could I explain?* I decided to go for the laugh.

"Yes, riding is very relaxing."

She didn't laugh, or even smile. I wanted to kill myself. *Is this how she thought I normally rode?* I couldn't think of a way to explain my actions that wouldn't take a considerable amount of time and possibly make the situation worse. I didn't say anything. She continued to be polite and talk to me in the future. Maybe it didn't look or sound as bad as I thought. Maybe.

After her month of rest, Penny was clearly in one of her "sound" phases. However, after seeing the X-rays, receiving the diagnosis, and discussing her affliction, I knew it would not, could not, be a permanent condition. Nothing changed the fact that this was a progressive disease we were dealing with, and it had already become severe.

That fact weighed heavily on my heart and nagged at my mind. As long as Penny had good stretches and we could take the edge off her pain with painkillers when she didn't, I was happy to keep things as they were. Although I knew where this was going, I didn't know how much time we were dealing with. I started to do some research. Nothing I read was encouraging. I decided to just let things run their course, as they inevitably would anyway.

This was one of the few times when Rich and I were not on the same page. We didn't discuss it because it was too depressing. However, Rich was on a search—actually, more of a quest. Every book, every article, on the computer was read and reread while he evaluated Penny's chances. He was determined to find a way to help her.

We were buying our hay at a stable that raised, trained, and showed Morgan horses. The owner, who seemed like a quiet man, was actually a bit of a jokester with a quick and dry wit. It was impossible not to like him. He also ran the equestrian program at the University of Connecticut and was involved with Connecticut's horse rescue program. Fate had thrown us together with one of the most knowledgeable horsemen in the area. His name is John Bennett.

When we got hay, we would pull a flat trailer and load about a hundred or more bales at a time. The bales would be stacked four or five rows high and had to be strapped down. I always helped Rich unload the trailer. I would scramble to the top row and, one by one, lower or roll a bale down to him. He would stack them in the barn. I went with him to get the hay, too. The idea was that I would help on that end as well. I really tried hard not to. It was like building the barn all over again. It was hard, sweaty work. The bales were heavy, and I had a hard time lifting them over my head.

Usually, it was Rich and John who loaded the trailer. I tried to look busy fussing with the straps. I'm positive I wasn't fooling anyone. It was during one of these loadings that I started to complain about the situation with Penny.

"She's just too young to be that lame, John." I was whining again. But, this time, I felt I was justified.

"How old is she?"

"Well, they said she was about six when we got her, and we've had her for close to four years now. I guess she's about ten. She has navicular syndrome, but it seems like there should be something we could do besides 'nerving' her. It seems like someone should have come up with something."

"Ten is awfully young," John concurred sympathetically.

"And there are people who can help," Rich said.

That stopped me cold. I had no idea what Rich was talking about.

"We have a horse that has navicular, and he's doing really well with special shoeing," John continued.

"Is he out of pain?" I asked.

"Certainly seems to be."

"Can he be ridden?"

"Sure, he's not only being ridden, but he's being shown at horse shows."

"Can we see him?" My heart was now doing cartwheels in my chest.

"Of course."

That was when we met Redford, a beautiful chestnut gelding. I stared as John lifted a front foot so I could see the bottom. The shoe was built up, and the center was deep, much, much deeper than a normal shoe.

"I was going to have him nerved. I didn't know what else to do. But our veterinarian said she thought that she and a farrier she works with might be able to help him. And they did."

"Any chance that your veterinarian is Dr. Elizabeth Maloney and the farrier is Danny Dunson?" Rich asked.

"Sure is. How do you know about them?" That was John's question, but I was wondering, too.

"I read about them on the Internet." Now Rich paused. I had a feeling as to what was coming. Rich doesn't like to ask for favors, but at least John was the type of person who made it easy. "If we brought Penny over here, do you think they would look at her?"

"I don't see why not. Do you have a horse trailer?"

Rich assured him that we did.

"They come once a month to do some of my horses, and other people in the area bring their horses if they need this kind of special shoeing. I'll ask my daughter Kay the next time they are due to come. She runs the stable. Then I'll call you. If you can bring Penny over, I'm sure they'll look at her."

On the ride home with the hay, I delivered my version of the Spanish Inquisition to my husband.

"Who are these people? How do you know about them? Do you really think they can help Penny? Why didn't you tell me about them? Where do they come from? How come I never read anything about them? Are they local?"

"The veterinarian is fairly local. She's from Massachusetts and specializes in lameness. The farrier she works with is from Tennessee. From what I read, he flies in about once a month and goes to some of the larger stables in New England. The vet evaluates the horse and X-rays its legs. Then she discusses it with the farrier. They decide on a course of treatment, including custom-making the shoes, right then and there. I didn't tell you because I didn't think this was an option for us. Danny only goes to the larger stables. He travels with a lot of equipment and a crew. I never got the impression they would travel to see just one horse. So I didn't know how to approach them."

And we never would have, if it hadn't been for John Bennett. John was true to his word. He called and told us when we could bring Penny over for examination. He said his daughter Kay had talked to the veterinarian and the farrier, so they would be expecting us. Kay would become

a big part of our lives. When I first met her, I was struck by her whole-
some beauty, what you would call the all-American girl.

The weather had turned bitterly cold and Penny was in even worse
condition than she had been when we took her to the out of state hospital. . She was lame in all four legs again, and she lay down for protracted
periods of time. She wouldn't lie flat but rather on her belly, with her legs
curled beneath her. Raz took to standing guard over her as she reclined.
She was very protective. However, the electric fence stayed on. I don't believe in my heart that Raz would have tried to hurt her at this point. But
if she tried, Penny couldn't even run away. Better safe than sorry. For all
of us.

One positive during this time was Penny's personality. She was so
used to being handled by people—poked and prodded—that she was
much calmer. Since she couldn't be ridden, I started brushing her more
to have more time with her. Like a lot of horses, she had a "tickle spot," a
spot on their body that, if you tickled just right, would make them laugh.
Penny's spot was under her head, where her head and neck met. For a lot
of horses, it is someplace on their bellies. And, of course, some can't, or
won't, be tickled at all.

Horses can't make the vocal sound of a laugh, but they will throw
their heads in the air. Although no noise comes out, it is obvious they are
delighted. Lately, however, I couldn't get this reaction out of Penny, no
matter how hard I tried. She was in so much pain I guess nothing seemed
very funny anymore. She also started resisting picking up her feet. She
didn't want to shift her weight onto the other legs. They all hurt.

As we loaded Penny on the trailer to take her to John's, Raz called
out pathetically. Penny whinnied back a couple of times, but then settled
in. Our neighbors would tell us later that Raz never did. She called and
cried out continuously until we returned late that night with Penny.

Once at the stable, we unloaded Penny and led her into the barn.
John and Kay were waiting for us, so were Veterinarian Elizabeth Maloney
and Farrier Danny Dunson. Also present was the veterinarian's assistant
and two men who worked with the farrier. This was quite an assemblage

for our little red horse. I noted Liz's (as we came to know her) portable X-ray machine and a trailer load of equipment that was Danny's.

We had brought all of our records, including a ton of paperwork and X-rays. Liz carefully went over everything. She then had us take Penny in the indoor ring and walk her around. She only had her move for a couple of minutes. She and Danny exchanged looks, and they told us to stop. We went back to the barn, and Liz took several X-rays of Penny's front legs. She used her portable, digital-computed radiography unit that transmitted the X-rays to her digital laptop. That way they could be viewed and printed immediately and on the spot.

As the pictures began to appear on the laptop, Liz shook her head and sighed, "Well, I always said I like a challenge."

John leaned over and studied them. "I think some of my horses have had worse than this."

Before I had a chance to get my hopes up by what John had said, Liz added,

"There is an additional problem with this horse. She has bone spurs on the navicular bone."

The bone spurs! We had known about them from the beginning. They are easy to pick up on X-rays. What we didn't know was that they were connected to the navicular disease. Apparently, not all navicular horses get bone spurs, and not all bone spurs are from navicular disease. Penny's unfortunately were. Liz went over and talked to Danny and then came back to us.

"What are you goals for Penny?"

"We want to stop or at least alleviate her pain as much as possible," Rich replied.

"And we want her to have at least some quality of life," I added.

"What would you consider a good quality of life for her?"

"Well, obviously as little pain as possible, but…" I hesitated here, but felt I had to go on. "Penny is a horse that loves to run. Now she lies on her belly all day. She is losing interest in everything. She's smart; that's just not her. It seems like a crummy life." I blurted this out in spite of myself, but I felt it was really important to be honest with these people. So I also added, "We may be exaggerating about how much pain she's in.

It is hard to tell. A veterinarian once told me she wasn't that bad because she was able to get up and down easily and often."

Danny spoke for the first time. "You're not wrong. Your horse is in a tremendous amount of pain. She's definitely circling the drain."

I felt my face go pale. I saw a mirror image of my distress in Rich's expression.

Liz tried to explain. "I think what that particular vet was thinking of was a horse with joint problems. They would definitely have a problem getting up, especially if it was in the knees. But Penny is what we call a footsore horse. All of her pain is in her feet, and it is considerable. The navicular disease has progressed to the point where she has little blood flow left to her front feet. The bone is starting to degenerate. There is hardly any circulation."

For a beat, nobody said anything.

Then Liz added, "What if we could help her, but she could never be ridden again?"

"Then she would never be ridden again," Rich and I said simultaneously.

"There are a lot of things we can do, both Danny and I, that haven't been tried on her yet. I can't guarantee anything. Each case is different, and some of it has to depend on the horse. Worse case scenario, we can remove a good deal of the pain. Best case, you might be able to ride her at some point in the future."

"If you can help her at all, she'll help herself. We've seen her do it over and over again." I couldn't leave it at that, though, and followed through with the question that had been plaguing me since our hospital trip, "But if you can't help—and I know you aren't guaranteeing you can—and if her quality of life isn't any better, would you…I mean, could you consider…"

"Putting her down?" Liz finished for me.

"Um, that's what I was getting at."

"Absolutely. I don't believe in keeping animals alive just so they can suffer. If physically and mentally she isn't any better and doesn't have a *reasonable* hope of improving, I would honor your request."

Rich was silent throughout this exchange. I wondered if he was starting to hate me. Well, I might as well seal the deal. I stated what I thought had to be said after seeing all these people and all the cutting-edge technology they had brought with them.

"I'd like to say that money is no object, but I can't—"

This was interrupted by a loud roar of laughter from Danny. "Thank God, because, in our experience, people who say they aren't worried about the money usually don't pay. Guess that's why they don't worry."

Liz was smiling now, too. "It's obvious how much money and love you've already invested in your horse. If you want us to proceed, we will work with you on the cost."

Okay, that was out of the way. Now I only had one more question that was going to make me uncomfortable, but I felt I had to ask it anyway.

"Is there a possibility that what you do could make her worse?"

Danny was obviously a very intelligent man, but he liked to play up his Tennessee hillbilly accent for humor, and he did that now.

"Well, darlin', you've got a horse with four bad legs. Unless she grows a fifth, and that one goes lame, too, I don't see how we can hurt her."

We all broke out laughing. However, before we could agree to anything, Danny had his own rule we had to willingly follow.

"A lot of people don't like their horses tranquilized. This is very exacting work, and I'm going to be spending a lot of time under this little gal. I know she seems really calm, but I won't work on her if I can't tranquilize her."

"Do whatever you have to do to keep the situation as safe as possible for everybody. We would never second-guess you on something like that. We don't have as much experience as some, but we've been around horses long enough to see a situation go south in a hurry. They're big animals," Rich replied. "Do what you need to do."

I nodded in agreement.

Kay would tell us privately that, in the course of his work, Danny had his back broken by a horse. He also had both his legs broken in different incidences. Tranquilized or not, I'm surprised he would still go near a horse. I wouldn't.

We agreed to proceed. Liz gave Penny a mild tranquilizer. She stood upright, but her eyes started to look drowsy. Danny and his assistants removed Penny's shoes. They were already assembling the replacements in their trailer. Both Liz and Danny agreed with the prior assessment of Penny's back legs. They felt that her back legs were basically sound and the lameness was being caused by the shift of weight from the front. Also, navicular disease is rarely seen in a horse's rear legs.

Once the new shoes were secured, Danny showed us how to treat the center of the shoes with an antibiotic dressing. This consisted of a mixture of granulated sugar and Betadine.

The new shoes totally supported the outside wall of the hooves. They were built up all the way around, but particularly in a way to remove pressure on the heal, where the pain was emanating from. The hole in the center of the shoe was packed with the Betadine mixture. That was held in place by a disposable baby diaper that was secured by duct tape. The duct tape covered the entire hoof, even the bottom. This made the dressing more resilient and able to last longer.

Rich and I watched carefully because it was made clear that this would have to be done three times a week. For the days in between the dressings, we were given a hoof-hardener to apply. Also, instead of the usual six- to eight-week cycle, Penny would have to have her shoes changed every month.

By this time, Penny was starting to perk up. She was still a little groggy, though, and we didn't want to trailer her until she had her balance. I asked John if I could walk Penny in the indoor ring until she was totally awake. He agreed immediately.

"Pick up your feet. Don't trip," I heard Rich call out as Penny and I walked away.

"Which one of them are you talking to?"

"Both of them."

"I heard that." I also heard the laughter that followed. I was smiling myself.

The shoeing was just the beginning of their plans for Penny. Liz also periodically injected Penny's ankles, something called Navicular Bursa injections. She would also try shockwave therapy, and we resumed giving Penny Cosequin for her joints. While none of this was inexpensive, true to their word, it never became so prohibitively expensive we couldn't afford it.

Penny's movements would have to be restricted again. By now, however, she had been in so much pain for so long she didn't fight it. As well as the pain, she was probably exhausted. Neither Rich nor I were expecting a cure. Navicluar is not a curable disease. We were not offered any expectations that it could be. But it sounded like it could be managed and at least buy our girl a longer and happier life.

After getting Penny settled back in, Rich and I went out to buy the supplies we needed. He went off to buy the Betadine and duct tape. I was in charge of the sugar and disposable diapers.

I found my way to the baby department in the nearest grocery store. When I stood in front of the diaper section, I realized how far the disposable diaper industry had come. When my children were babies, I had the choice between cloth or disposable. Now I was faced with a dizzying assortment of sizes, brands, and cartoon characters.

A stock boy approached. "Can I help you?"

"I hope so. I really don't know what size to get."

"How big?"

"Around ten."

"Months or pounds?"

"Years."

I turned and saw his stricken face. He must have thought I had a special needs or injured child.

"Oh, no, no. It's not what you're thinking. They're for my horse."

"Oh, okay. I have to go water the vegetables now."

"Sure, of course. Go ahead. I'll figure it out." I was talking to myself. He had already beaten a hasty retreat.

Well, that was awkward. And what did he mean he had to "water the vegetables"? However, considering my end of the conversation, I figured I couldn't afford to be snotty. I grabbed a couple of boxes of the newborn size and left the store. I made sure to use another store the next time I needed them.

Once the new treatments and new shoes began, there was an almost immediate change in Penny. We were keeping her in a smaller area as instructed, but she didn't seem to mind much. She was perkier, though, and wasn't lying down as often. Our hopes were to relieve most of her pain. Dr. Maloney was present at almost every shoeing and continued to tweak the angle and also suggest other types of treatment for relief.

Rich and I were both working. This had to be done every four weeks. If it hadn't been for John and his daughter Kay, it would have been impossible for us to keep that schedule. Kay would call and let us know when Danny was expected. She also offered to let Penny be brought in a day or two ahead of schedule, to make it more convenient for us. One of us tried to be at every shoeing, but we couldn't do that and keep our jobs. If a snowstorm was expected, we would bring her even earlier. They would not accept payment, saying they had the room anyway.

Only a couple of months into treatment, Liz saw a huge improvement. She told me I could start riding Penny again, but only at a walk or trot. I was ecstatic.

Kay gave lessons in a large outdoor ring, and Rich and I began regular weekly lessons. I was afraid that we wouldn't recognize it if Penny was being too active. Kay had experience with several horses with similar problems, and I knew she would know how hard I could ride Penny. Or perhaps I should say how much I could let Penny go. She was back to pushing the limits on every ride, and I couldn't count on her to slow down, not even because of pain. And, frankly, Raz needed a little professional guidance as well. We couldn't tell if she was being "difficult" or we were expecting too much of her. Kay helped us with all of that. Only then did we realize how good both these horses could be.

The winter was more difficult because any horse with problem legs shouldn't be ridden in a small indoor arena. The frequent turning puts too much of a strain on them. Both horses got less exercise. I was getting to the point where I didn't want to ride in freezing weather, indoors or out, anyway.

With the approach of Christmas, Penny took a sharp turn for the worse. We had one giant snowstorm, and another was on the way. The roads were barely plowed. We called Liz, and she said she could meet us at John's. We loaded Penny in the trailer and started the short trek to Connecticut and what we hoped would be some answers and help. I fretted that these treatments weren't going to work anymore or that I had let her hurt herself. The road was horrible, and we weren't more than a couple of miles from home when a huge diesel snowplow approached us from the opposite direction. Rich hugged our side of the road as much as possible, but there really was no place to go. The plow hit us and sent both truck and trailer into the ditch. It wasn't a violent crash (we were practically stopped), but it sure put us in a tough spot.

There were no houses on that side of the road, just forest. We got out immediately to check on Penny. She seemed okay, a little hyper, but that was to be expected. We decided to unload her while Rich tried to get back on the road. Once I had her unloaded and standing in the middle of the road, Rich surveyed the situation and said something I've never heard him say before.

"Sand, I don't know if I can get this out of here. We're in really deep."

My blood ran cold. We had to get this horse to Connecticut. Rich is an excellent driver and an optimist to boot. But he wasn't omnipotent. *And what would we do if he couldn't get back on the road?* I heard the plow returning. He hadn't meant to hit us, and he was coming back to help. The diesel made Penny even more excitable.

People had started emerging from the house across the street. One of the men had chains. I walked over to a woman and asked if I could put Penny in their driveway. She agreed immediately and even suggested bringing her to the back of the house so she wouldn't be so close to the action. I was wearing my rubber barn boots and was slipping all over the place. Every time Penny moved in one direction or the other, I would land on my knees. It had started snowing again. I couldn't see if any progress was being made with the truck.

The woman approached politely with her children. They asked if they could pat Penny. I was glad that Penny's personality had gotten so mellow, because I sure didn't have control over her and the situation was a mess. How could I say no when we were standing, by their good graces, on their property? I felt pretty confident in giving the go ahead. Penny stood still for the patting, even reveled in it. The snow came down on her bright-red coat, and snowflakes caught on her long lashes that encircled her soft, brown eyes—a fact that did not escape her new admirers. They gushed about how beautiful and friendly she was. She really did look amazing.

Rich came around the corner of the house to tell me the truck and trailer, with the help or our Good Samaritans, were back on the road and we could load Penny again.

At his approach, Penny jerked her head violently, and I was sent sprawling into the snow. I felt my eyes fill with tears and snow as I worried about what would be at the end of this trip. I was cold, tired, and discouraged. The woman—and I'm embarrassed that I never got her or any of their names—leaned over to where I was trying to get up off my knees. She seemed oblivious to my predicament.

"I just wanted to thank you," she said. "None of us have ever been this close to a horse, never mind patted one. And she is just so beautiful. You've made this a very memorable Christmas for us."

I glanced at her sincere expression and tried to keep even a hint of sarcasm out of my voice when I replied, "Yes, it really is." (I was struggling for words and calm.) "I mean, it really has been...um...magical."

Rich and I thanked everyone, I got Penny loaded back on the trailer, and we started out again. Only now we had a dent in the truck.

When we got to the Bennetts', Kay and Liz were waiting for us. The good news was Penny's lameness didn't seem to have anything to do with navicular. It appeared she had another abscess, this time in her right front leg.

We knew what that meant—soaking her foot several times a day and then applying the dressing of disposable diapers and duct tape. Although soaking Penny's foot was no longer a challenge, this would still make things difficult for us. The storm was still predicted, and Christmas was coming. *If we took her home, would we be able to get her to help if something went wrong?* It seemed like Kay was reading our minds.

"Would you like to leave her here? I can soak her foot while I'm taking care of the other horses and then put the dressing on." This was a hugely generous offer, and I can't tell you what it meant to us. "The only thing," Kay said hesitantly, "is Christmas. I have plans, and I wouldn't be able to take care of her treatment."

We rushed to reassure her that would be fine. We could take care of her on Christmas Day, and we did. We also asked what it would cost to leave Penny with them for several days and for all the time and work that Kay would be expending. She and her dad refused payment. He said they had the room anyway. We argued, and he finally agreed to what amounted to a negligible payment. Kay wouldn't budge at all. She said she was there anyway and refused any type of reimbursement. How do you repay that kind of selflessness? The only answer Rich and I came up with is you can't. We will always owe them for this and countless other acts of kindness they extended to us over those years.

The spring after this incident, Penny improved immensely. After examining her, Liz gave me the go ahead to lope her. I just had to keep the lope reasonably slow and on good footing. Rich and I decided to go to the Bennetts' every week for more lessons. That way we knew the footing would be the best and we had Kay's eyes as well as our own to watch for any red flags from Penny.

After a couple of weeks of conditioning, I started to lope Penny again. It felt marvelous. I had forgotten how smoothly she moved. For a couple of weeks, we would walk, trot, and then lope a circuit at the end of the hour. Raz would make this circle several times, but we held Penny to one to start off with. Since we didn't see any ill effects, we decided to try to lengthen Penny's loping time. This was an oblong enclosure, with two long sides and the shorter sides on the end. I loped Penny around once, with both Kay and Rich watching to see if she appeared to be struggling. Once I completed the first lap, I glanced at Kay without slowing, and she gave me a "go ahead" nod.

I let Penny lope a second time, and although I was putting some pressure on the reins, I couldn't help but notice her speed increasing. We had completed a second lap and were starting on a third when I felt Penny gather herself and at the same time begin pulling on the bit. She was going for it—an all-out gallop at top speed—if I let her. I didn't dare. I was afraid she would hurt herself, and I immediately pulled her to a stop. At one point in time she would have bolted, and I wouldn't have been able to stop her. A lot had happened since then. We were soul mates now, and she listened and did what I asked, even if she didn't want to.

Rich and Kay walked over to where we had stopped.

I said to them, "I think she was trying to break into a gallop."

"She was definitely going for it," They both said, almost in unison.

"You did the right thing in stopping her; we don't want to take a chance," Kay said, and then she added, "Wait until I tell Liz; she'll be thrilled. She really has some speed in her, doesn't she?" Indeed she did.

The really encouraging part about this incident was Penny wasn't on any pain medication that day and hadn't been for quite a while. She hadn't been frightened or spooked. So we could rule out an adrenaline rush. And she had been warmed up properly and allowed to gradually increase her speed, not encouraged to. She must have been feeling well enough to do it. There was only one thing that made me a little cautious about celebrating just yet: Penny's absolute love of running. She hadn't been pushed, but was just allowed to enjoy herself up to a point.

That was a good summer. We stayed cautious, but Penny and I got to lope more regularly. This was something I didn't think she would be able to do again. I was able to be there the next time she was shod. I couldn't help but thank Liz and give her a hug.

"I never thought we could get this far! And we couldn't have if it wasn't for you. And Danny. Uh, and Kay and John."

Liz laughed and said, "Well, you know what they say; it takes a village."

She was pleased at Penny's progress and always remembered to include Penny when giving out credit. "She's an amazing girl. She has a great heart. We couldn't help her if she didn't help herself."

The summer progressed, and although there were the occasional ups and downs, it was more than we could have hoped for. Penny was back to being playful, with us and with Raz. Occasionally, we had to decrease her half of the paddock so she didn't hurt herself.

Winter came, and we were all forced to take it easy. I was now making plans in my head. I was contemplating the idea of riding bareback. Penny had become so responsive that I trusted her enough for the first time to attempt to ride without a saddle. This wasn't an exercise in vanity. I was searching for ways to try to take the stress off her legs. I thought if I could eliminate my heavy Western saddle that might help. I discussed the possibility with Kay. At my age, I really didn't want to take too many more falls. I didn't know if what I was planning was practical.

Kay thought it was very doable. She said Penny and I had a bond. I was right to trust her. There had been occasions when something unexpected spooked the horses. All I had to do was put my hand on Penny's neck and tell her it would be okay. She may have flinched, but that was all. Raz had her usual nervous breakdown, but Rich is a strong rider and could handle it. In fairness to Raz, she wasn't getting half the attention we all lavished on Penny—not because Penny was the favorite, but because she needed it.

That spring started out well. Penny was in good spirits, and that made us all happy. I planned on getting her in shape and then trying to ditch the saddle. Rich and I had discussed my retiring early. That would give us both time to do more riding. We included Kay in our plans, and she happily mentioned having a retirement party for me.

That's when things started to go downhill. Penny threw a shoe and immediately went dead lame. We got the shoe put back on the same day, but it appeared the damage was done. Liz prescribed stall rest for Penny. We kept her quiet for as long as recommended, but she seemed sick of the whole deal by now. When we finally loaded her up to take her to Kay's for a lesson, she started to relentlessly kick the trailer. She had never done that before. She had always been excellent in the trailer. By the time we got to

Connecticut, she was lame again, this time in her rear legs. She had given them a tremendous pounding.

You could see the blue paint from the trailer on her back hooves. There were also considerable dents in the trailer itself. More rest for Penny. She began lying down again.

She wasn't bouncing back. We asked Liz to examine her. The words "progressive disease" bounced around in my head.

Rich, Kay, and I grouped around Liz as she took new X-rays of Penny's front feet. She frowned at the image of Penny's right front foot. She took another X-ray from another angle. Then she took it again. She frowned again at the images as they appeared on her laptop. She took one more.

Then she sighed and said, "I'm taking so many X-rays because I want to rule out any anomalies caused by the machine. It's not the machine. Do you see those white spots?"

We all nodded.

"Those are new bone spurs. They've grown into the deep flexor tendon. Now when Penny runs, she could—will tear that tendon. They're going to keep growing. Eventually, it will tear if she even moves."

"What about surgery?" Rich asked. "You know, to remove the bone spurs?"

"I know how you guys feel about this horse. Any surgery of this type would be tremendously expensive. But if I thought it had a chance of success, I would tell you to raid your 401K or do whatever you want to do to afford it. The fact is, though, this kind of surgery doesn't exist. Even if it did, the bone would just come back. That's how far the disease has progressed. I'm afraid this is a game ender."

Neither Rich nor I had the right to be surprised. We had been kept informed the entire time; however, that didn't lessen the blow. We were silent.

Liz turned and looked at us. "You know it has been a miracle that Penny has done as well as she has for as long as she has?"

We both nodded.

Looking at me, she said, "But you'd like just one more miracle?"

"Yes, please."

Liz had a sad smile when she turned away and looked at the X-rays one more time. "I guess we could keep her on pain medication for a while and see how she does."

It was clear that, although it's not what she wanted, she was fresh out of miracles. I felt Rich squeeze my hand and Kay's arm around my shoulder. We all held our positions for a few seconds, frozen in time. We had to let our minds struggle to comprehend the thing we dreaded most.

"You don't have to make any decisions right now. Like I said, we can keep her comfortable with pain medication for a time..."

All four of us knew there really wasn't any decision to be made. Now it was just a matter of attending to the details.

"We've never lost a horse. I don't even know how to go about it."

"I'll take care of the medical part of it," said Liz.

"You can bury her here on our property. I'll check with my dad, but I'm sure it will be okay," added Kay.

We left Penny with Kay and went home. Even though there were no choices to be made, no options to be had, Rich and I discussed it. We discussed it and discussed it and discussed it. Our minds raced around with the idea, like rats in maze, looking for a way out that didn't exist. The summer was ending; the thought of dealing with Penny in crisis in the middle of winter was daunting. More importantly, it wouldn't change anything. We could prolong things, maybe, for a short time. We couldn't stop them. We knew from experience that there was only one thing left to do.

We agreed on the inevitable, because in the end, what else can you do? I called Kay and told her we would have Penny put down. My voice was shaking, and I was borderline incoherent. Kay understood, and we agreed on a date. She told me she would tell Liz. She asked if we would be there.

Rich and I had discussed this. I thought at least one of us should be there so Penny wouldn't be frightened, but I didn't know if I could do it. Rich seemed to have no doubts.

"If you feel you need to be there, I understand. But, Sandy, I can't. I just can't watch that."

I didn't think less of him for this decision. As a matter of fact, I admired him for being able to make it. I didn't know what I would do. I felt terribly torn between duty and wanting to remember Penny the way she looked when she was running free with her neck arched and her tail held high.

"Rich has to work, Kay, but I think I will…I mean, I should be there."

"You don't have to come, Sandy. Penny knows Liz, and she knows me. She won't be alone. She won't be frightened. I promise you. Also, you can change your mind at any time. That would be okay with both Liz and me."

I thanked Kay, and we chose the following Monday for a date. I hung up without committing one way or another as to where I would be that morning.

Raz was already going crazy without Penny. She was calling out constantly, and it didn't look like she would be stopping anytime soon. I had told Kay about the situation, and as usual, she had help at hand.

"Why not take Shelby home for a while? No one will ride her now, and she would benefit from a little one-on-one attention. You could keep her until you find another horse, or until Raz calms down."

Shelby Jean was a beautiful little Morgan horse. She was in her early twenties and recently had to have an eye removed at Tufts. She was acting depressed, and I had always had a soft spot for her. She was a little pistol who was usually full of energy, but very friendly and easy to handle. Now she seemed despondent in her stall, staring vacantly at the wall. I knew how she felt. I agreed to take her.

Rich and I went up to see Penny and pick up Shelby Jean. I saw John staring at us from across the street. I wondered if he thought we were giving up too easily. He was an excellent horseman. I felt guilty anyway; now I wondered if he was judging us. Rich was with Penny, and I was talking to Shelby Jean (I know how it sounds, but I *was* talking to her) when I heard John come up behind me.

"You're doing the right thing, you know," John said softly.

I hadn't realized I was holding my breath until I exhaled.

"When Kay told me and asked if you could bury Penny here, I said, 'The Packards are good people. We'll do whatever we can to make it easier for them.' You guys can pick any spot you want, Sandy. You can put up a marker if you like." John then told me about the first horse he loved and lost. About how it was an unremarkable horse and didn't seem particularly special to anyone—except to him. It was special to him. He ended the conversation with a reassuring hug. How was it that I still doubted our decision? I don't know, but I did.

That Saturday I had made plans to go shopping and have lunch with our daughter. I hadn't intended on telling Annie at that time. I hadn't even known what was going to happen when we had made our plans. As the day went on, however, Penny was never out of my mind. Before Annie could leave, I blurted it out. She was surprised. We had never really gone into the details of Penny's problems with her. She had been a veterinarian technician for about eleven years at that point. She was then going to school and working part time.

"Have you ever seen a horse die, Annie?" I thought she might have in the course of her work.

"No, not a horse," she said hesitantly. "Are you and Dad going to be there?"

"Dad has to work. I don't know if I'm going. I don't know if I can."

"When is it going to happen?"

"This coming Monday, at ten a.m."

"I don't have anything to do Monday. I'll come to your house and go with you."

"Annie, I don't want you to drive all the way over to our house, when I may decide not to go. It's going to happen whether I'm there or not. There will be good people with her."

"I have nothing to do Monday, so I'll just come over and be with you. You can decide if you want to go or not then. Do you honestly think I would get upset if I drove to your house and you decided you didn't want to watch your horse die?" She said this with a soft smile on her lips and a huge lie in her heart. I knew she had plenty to do on Monday between school and work. We had to plan for weeks just to get this Saturday together. I didn't call her on it, though, because in truth, the idea of her support was so appealing. She's a good person to have in a bad situation. I didn't want to lose that.

Monday arrived and so did Annie. We left for Connecticut and Penny, just like Annie knew we would. On the drive there, I remembered I had a silver angel pin that I wanted to tie in Penny's mane with a ribbon. I had left it at home. I slowed the car and explained to Annie.

"Are you going back for it?"

We were halfway there. It wasn't a long trip, but I knew if I went back, I probably couldn't get up the nerve to set out a second time. I didn't turn around. I sped up and resumed our journey.

"No, I'm not going back. I don't think it's necessary."

"You're right. It's not necessary. It's the thought that counts. And, Mom, it was a really nice thought."

We arrived at the stable. I knew John couldn't be there; he had told me that when we picked up Shelby Jean. Liz hadn't arrived yet. Kay was giving a lesson. I was a little surprised to see Danny's equipment in front of the barn. Then I remembered this was his normal week to shoe the horses in this area. Annie and I started to walk over to Penny's stall.

"Hey, Sandy, can I see you for a minute?" It was Danny.

My heart dropped. *Did he have an idea that might or might not help Penny? Or was he judging us and finding us lacking?* I reluctantly turned to meet him. I couldn't take this roller coaster ride much longer. I went to go around the back of the barn so I wouldn't be between him, his assistants, and the horses they were working on.

"No, no," he said, "come right through here."

"I didn't want to be in the way," I said as I approached him.

Danny smiled kindly. "Today you can't be in the way. I just wanted to tell you—and I would appreciate it if you would tell Rich—that I admire you guys. You're doing the right thing. You're putting your horse before yourselves. A lot of people don't do that. You've done everything possible. And now you're doing the kind thing."

"Are you sure, Danny? Are you sure it's the right thing?"

"Of course I am. I've been working with you guys for what—two and a half, three years now? It's obvious how much you love your horse. And she loves and trusts you. Her pain will be over forever in a few minutes. You guys will be hurting for a long time. I know you will."

His words hit home and made sense. Or maybe it was just the final vote of support after so much positive reinforcement. We hugged, and I joined Annie at Penny's stall. Kay finished giving her lesson and came over.

"I gave her some pain meds this morning."

We had to be careful about pain medication because, in the long term, they can have harsh side effects. That was no longer an issue. There would be no long term. Keeping her as pain free as possible only made sense. I thanked Kay. I didn't even ask what she had given Penny. I knew she would have discussed it with Liz. I saw Liz's car pull up. Kay said Liz wanted to check a horse that Danny was shoeing, and then they would join us. I asked if we could take Penny in the meadow and let her graze. She said of course and left to join Liz.

Annie, Penny, and I crossed the street to where there was lush green grass. Penny was alert, friendly, and moving relatively easily.

"Gee," Annie exclaimed, "she doesn't seem that lame."

I started to explain about the pain medication, and I could see a knowing look dawn on her. She got it; I didn't have to explain further.

The sun was warm; it was a beautiful day. Penny's grave had been dug by a backhoe on the other side of a stone wall. We couldn't see it from where we were. We watched a coyote lope across the field. One of the girls that worked part time at the stable came over to us.

"Do you mind?" she asked. "I promised everyone at the barn I would do something today."

I nodded my okay, but didn't know what she meant.

She stepped in close to Penny and raised Penny's head with her hands. Then she planted a kiss on Penny's nose.

"Do you mind if I stay?"

"No, of course not." It occurred to me that Penny would have more friends at her funeral than some people.

Liz and Kay appeared. I introduced Annie all around. Then I asked Liz if I could pay her then instead of after. It occurred to me I might not be in great emotional shape after.

"I'm not charging you, Sandy. I wouldn't consider this a practice-building endeavor."

"You could just send me a bill..."

She shook her head negatively. Kay and John had also refused any attempt on our part to give them money. Somewhere along the line, our relationship transcended the financial.

The five of us walked behind the stone wall to the grave. I stood Penny beside it, and Liz gave her a tranquilizer. I stroked Penny's neck as her eyes grew heavy. The sun was warm, and Penny looked like she was drifting off to sleep. I didn't want to let go of her halter. I knew the drug to euthanize her was next. I saw Liz fidget.

"Would this be a good time for us to leave?" I meant Annie and me. I didn't want to see Penny fall.

"Well, she won't notice if you leave right now. If we wait much longer, I'll have to tranquilize her again."

I gave Penny's lovely neck one last stroke, and Annie and I walked down the hill.

Annie drove us home; my hands were shaking too much to drive. It occurred to me how lucky I was to have her. Kay called that night to assure me that everything had continued smoothly. Penny never totally shook off the effects off the tranquilizer. She hadn't seen us leave.

I hadn't intended on making this sad. Neither Rich nor I ever regretted for one minute our time with Penny. And because of her, we have become friends with some amazing people. But sometimes life is so bittersweet you just can't edit out the sad parts. At least I can't.

www.ingramcontent.com/pod-product-compliance
Lightning Source LLC
Chambersburg PA
CBHW060310290526
45789CB00001B/470